MURDERING MOMMY

HORRIFYING TALES OF CHILDREN WHO KILLED THEIR OWN MOTHERS

WILLIAM WEBB

Absolute Crime Press
ANAHEIM, CALIFORNIA

Copyright © 2019 by Minute Help, Inc.

All rights reserved. No part of this publication may be reproduced, distributed or transmitted in any form or by any means, including photocopying, recording, or other electronic or mechanical methods, without the prior written permission of the publisher, except in the case of brief quotations embodied in critical reviews and certain other noncommercial uses permitted by copyright law.

Contents

About Absolute Crime 1

Introduction 3

Mary Lamb 5

Sidney Harry Fox 15

Jack Gilbert Graham 24

Charles Whitman 35

John Emil List 47

Antony Baekeland 58

Brett Reider 69

The Menendez Brothers 78

Aaron Brown 88

Dr. Idella Kathleen Hagen 98

Luke Woodham 109

Kip Kinkel 118

Alyssa Bustmante: Teenaged Thrill Killer and Church Goer 129

Ronald Joseph "Butch" DeFeo, Jr. 138

Edmund Kemper 148

ABOUT ABSOLUTE CRIME

Absolute Crime publishes only the best true crime literature. Our focus is on the crimes that you've probably never heard of, but you are fascinated to read more about. With each engaging and gripping story, we try to let readers relive moments in history that some people have tried to forget.

Remember, our books are not meant for the faint at heart. We don't hold back--if a crime is bloody, we let the words splatter across the page so you can experience the crime in the most horrifying way!

If you enjoy this book, please visit our homepage to see other books we offer; if you have any feedback, we'd love to hear from you!

Dear reader, your heart may not be able to handle the shocking true facts presented in this humble volume. You have been warned.

Introduction

It's not unusual for someone to have issues with their parents, but the 15 cases profiled in this book show that sometimes they can't be resolved with a conversation. In some cases, frequent physical and metal abuse led to murder, while other cases were just mentally deranged people taking out their frustrations on the closest person available.

These short profiles show what happens when sons and daughters snap and end the lives of those who brought them into this world.

MARY LAMB

Introduction

Mary Ann Lamb was an English writer and sister of Charles Lamb, also a famous writer, best known for his work, Essays of Elia. She is perhaps most remembered for her joint collaboration on the Tales of Shakespeare, which she co-wrote with Charles. Mary Ann was plagued off and on throughout her life with mental health issues and spent many years in mental hospitals. In 1796, during one of her repeated mental breakdowns, Mary Ann Lamb stabbed her mother to death.

Early Life

Born on December 3, 1764, to a poor family in London, England, Mary Ann Lamb was the third of seven children born to Elizabeth and John Lamb. Her inspiration to become a writer was probably most influenced by her father. While growing up, he told her stories about literature and writers, which piqued her interest in books.

During her childhood, Mary Ann attended day school in Holborn, England and she was a voracious reader. She was lucky enough to have access to an extensive library belonging to her father's employer. Although Mary Ann had little formal education beyond day school, she was able to help support her family by doing sewing and needlework to earn extra money.

What Drove Mary Ann Lamb to the Breaking Point?

Her father John Lamb suffered a stroke and passed away in 1799. Her mother Elizabeth began experiencing chronic pain and wound up becoming incapable of taking care of herself. Mary Ann was the only child remaining at home, so the responsibility of caregiving fell entirely upon her.

Sarah Lamb, her father's sister came to live with the family as she grew older, with Charles and Mary Ann taking turns caring for her. Charles suffered a mental breakdown in 1795 and spent the rest of the year, including the beginning of 1796, in a private mental hospital receiving care.

During the time when Mary Ann was a caregiver for her family members, she also began working as a seamstress and hired a young girl to act as her apprentice. The extra responsibilities and stress of taking care of everyone weighed quite heavily on Mary Ann and she began to experience the symptoms of a mental breakdown.

What Happened the Day Elizabeth Lamb Died?

On September 22, 1796, as she was preparing dinner, Mary Ann became angered by her apprentice. She roughly shoved the girl and pushed her from room to room, while loudly chastising her. Elizabeth Lamb began to yell continuously at Mary for becoming angry with her apprentice. Mary Ann was subject to anxiety attacks and due to extreme exhaustion from the constant caregiving, she reached her breaking point.

Mary Ann grabbed a kitchen knife and unsheathed it. She approached her mother who was in a seated position, took the knife and stabbed her directly in the heart, killing her instantly. Her father and aunt were witnesses to the incident and it was rumored he was injured during the attack. Charles ran into the room soon after the stabbing and removed the knife from his sister's hand.

Later, on the evening of the murder, Mary Ann was confined to a mental institution called Fisher House in Islington. Mary Ann's brother John suggested Charles have her committed to a public facility, but he refused and took over total responsibility, so she would not be permanently institutionalized. It was at this time that Mary Ann and Charles began to have a close and devoted relationship, which lasted until his death.

What Kind of Person was Mary Ann Lamb?

It can be said from reading past accounts about the life of Mary Ann Lamb that she was described as a loving, gentle and sweet person She had to have been a compassionate and giving person to uncomplainingly take on the burdens of caring for several incapacitated family members. Mary Ann was so desperate to help her family; she also worked her fingers to the bone as a seamstress in order to provide for everyone.

Mary Ann was ten years older than her brother Charles and was a sort of surrogate mother to him while he was growing up. The two siblings had a very close relationship and some of earliest sonnets written by Charles were about his sister. He wrote praising her selflessness, sweetness, compassion and enduring spirit.

What Happened to Mary Ann Lamb After her Mother's Murder?

Six months after murdering her mother, Mary Ann Lamb was removed from Fisher House by her brother Charles. He bought her a house in Hackney, located not far from London. After the death of her mother, Mary Ann was described by many as being lucid, warm and understanding. It was during the time following the death of her mother that Mary Ann started to hone her writing and poetry skills. She perfected her craft, even though she still experienced yearly relapses back into depression and required hospitalization many times.

While living in Hackney, Charles regularly visited his sister on Sundays and holidays, while the rest of the time he paid for her to have caregivers. Mary Ann continued working as a seamstress and frequented local lending libraries to feed her love of books. After her father and aunt died, Charles brought Mary Ann back to London to live with him full time. Both siblings agreed to remain together and not marry for the rest of their lives.

When Did Mary Ann Lamb Begin her Writing Career?

In 1801, Charles and Mary Ann Lamb formed a social and literary circle that counted artists and writers as members. Charles started to drink heavily and it became a problem that plagued him throughout his life. Mary took on the role of caregiver again; she nursed Charles through his hangovers and binges, watching over him just like he had done for her.

In 1806, when William Goodwin and his wife had become close to Mary Ann and Charles, he asked her to write something for their Juvenile Library. Mary Ann soon found she had a passion and love of writing for children, coming to realize she could earn a good living through being a writer.

Mary Ann began writing her collection of stories, Mrs. Leicester's School, in 1806; the book was published by the end of the year. In 1810, Mary Ann and Charles published another collaboration called Poems for Children; their joint writing efforts brought them financial security along with a new social stature.

What Happened to Mary Ann Lamb in Later Years?

Mary Ann wrote an article entitled "On Needle-work" in December of 1814. The piece was published by the New British Lady's Magazine under her pseudonym Sempronia. The article pushed for sewing and dressmaking to be recognized as a profession, making it more than just a duty women did as part of their daily chores. Around this time, Mary Ann experienced a relapse back into depression and Charles published the Essays of Elia. Charles wrote the book about his sister and her life, but the information was never revealed to the public.

Charles and Mary Ann met a young girl name Emma Isola in 1820; it is thought the introduction was made by William Wordsworth. During the time Emma lived with them, Charles resigned his job with the East India House and the three of them moved to a grand home in the country. Charles and Mary Ann later adopted Emma after her father passed away in 1823.

In the late 1820's, Mary Ann began to experience a progression of her mental illness and her periods of dementia lasted much longer than usual. In addition to experiencing a relapse in her mental illness, she also began having new symptoms and became detached from others. Charles's health also began to deteriorate; he became infirmed due to his rampant alcohol problem and other health conditions.

In 1833, Mary Ann Lamb moved to a sanitarium for the mentally ill and Charles soon followed her there. Even as she fell more deeply into mental illness, Charles never wavered in his love and dedication to his sister. Charles Lamb passed away on December 27, 1834 and according to a family friend, Mary Ann was so lost in insanity, she was never able to fully experience the grief and loss.

What is the Legacy of Mary Ann Lamb?

Mary Ann Lamb died on May 20, 1847 and was buried next to her brother Charles in the Edmonton Church graveyard in Middlesex, England. At the time of her death, there were very few people outside of her immediate family and close friends who knew the truth of her mental health issues or the murder of her mother.

There were people who remembered her in a positive light and focused more on her sweetness and gentility. However, there were others who focused on the negatives and did not remember her with fondness. For whatever she was, Mary Ann Lamb has left an interesting legacy that will surely be studied and pondered for many generations to come.

SIDNEY HARRY FOX

Introduction

Sidney Harry Fox was a British con man and swindler who left a trail of trouble wherever he went. Fox was not above using his homosexuality to turn a profit and it was rumored he engaged in sexual relationships with a number of older men. Although Sidney Harry Fox had a lengthy criminal record, his mother was always steadfastly by his side, never doubting his innocence. It seems there was almost nothing that Sidney Harry Fox would not do for money. He was accused and convicted of murdering his mother in order to collect money from her life insurance policy.

Who was Sidney Harry Fox?

Sidney Harry Fox was born in January of 1899 in Great Fransham, Norfolk. He was the fourth and youngest of son of Rosaline Rallison Fox. Rosaline married William George Fox, but left him for a railway porter who was rumored to be Sidney's biological father. Sidney Harry Fox grew up never knowing the true identity of his father and it was something that tortured him throughout his life.

Fox was educated at the parish school of Great Fransham, Norfolk, where he resided until he was 13-years old. Because of his illegitimacy, Fox was given to daydreaming about his father and this led him to fantasize about being of noble birth. For three years, Sidney worked in London for an Irish baron named Sir John Leslie and he soon became the pet of the family. He earned the nickname "Cupid" because of his disarming charm and natural good looks.

While living with the Leslie family, Fox started running a series of scams. He was able to seduce the family's elderly housemaid with his charms and made off with her life savings. Next on the list, Fox stole the Leslie family silver and bible, reportedly using the signatures in the book to engage in deceptive practices. After being disgraced, he went on to work as a ledger clerk in a bank, but was fired after stealing checkbooks.

Life from 1917-1922

Between 1917 and 1918, Sidney spent three months doing hard labor because of obtaining money under false pretenses. The epileptic seizures that had plagued Fox during his childhood began to reappear, landing him in the hospital for six months. The seizures, along with debilitating headaches rendered him unfit for employment.

Fox underwent medical evaluations and it was noted he was backward in development and simple minded. Another evaluation stated Sidney was alert, but suffered from an anxiety disorder. He became a clerk at the Grindlay Bank in July 1919, but within less than a month he had gone back to his old tricks of forgery and deceptive practices. As a consequence, Fox was sentenced to eight months of hard labor.

In 1920, Sidney was given six months of hard labor for using the name of a Harrods's customer to obtain a gold cigarette case and several expensive suits. Later in 1922, Fox received another twelve month sentence of hard labor for obtaining credit under fraudulent pretenses from a London Hotel. Throughout the later part of the 1920's, Sidney repeatedly spent time in jail for a variety of thefts, frauds and other petty crimes.

Homosexual Lifestyle

When he could, Fox would use his homosexuality to gain money and other favors. It is rumored Sidney engaged in sexual relationships with a variety of older men. On two occasions, officers wound up being disgraced when police found letters Fox had written to them. Scotland Yard described Sidney as having an unbridled penchant for men and a terrifying sexual history.

Fox became known in social circles as living off the wealth and kindness of other men, who should have known better. Sidney adored the company of older, wealthy gentlemen and enjoyed the theater environment. In 1925, James Agate came to admire Fox, describing him as debonair, charming and suave; he too was not immune to Sidney's charms.

Sidney Harry Fox and Mrs. Charlotte Isabel Morris

Around 1927, Fox became the lover of a married, middle-aged, Australian woman named Charlotte Isabel Morse. While with her, he stole her jewelry and took out a life insurance policy on her for approximately $20,000 USD. Mrs. Morse woke up one night from a sound sleep and found the gas tap had been turned on in her bedroom; it was an unsuccessful attempt by Sidney to end her life.

For the crime of stealing Charlotte's jewelry, Fox was imprisoned for fifteen months. In spite of his talent for smooth talking women, Sidney never wanted any of his male benefactors to find out about his relationship with Charlotte because of how it would appear.

Sidney Harry Fox and the Murder of Rosaline Fox

In 1929, after he was released from prison, Sidney rescued his mother Rosaline from the poorhouse in Portsmouth. The two started leading a precarious lifestyle of living in expensive hotel rooms while biding their time, waiting until the law caught up with them. Sidney doted on his mother and treated her well, until he came up with idea of profiting from her demise.

Around April of 1929, Sidney Harry Fox convinced his mother to make a will naming him as beneficiary, after he took out a large life insurance policy on her. On May 1, 1929 Fox took out a life insurance policy on his mother that was due to expire on October 23, 1929.

Several months later, Sidney and Rosaline arrived at the Margate hotel; they booked two rooms but did not bring any luggage.

At the time Sidney and Rosaline were staying at the Margate, there were two life insurance policies on her. The policies were renewed on October 21, 1929 and were worth several thousands of dollars each. On October 23, Fox and Rosaline had dinner; afterward he purchased a bottle of wine as a "nightcap" for his mother. At 11:30 p.m. that night, Sidney raised an alarm, stating there was a fire in Rosaline's suite. Her half-clothed body was pulled from the room by another hotel guest.

Although a doctor ruled Rosaline's death to be caused by suffocation and shock, insurance investigators examined the room and believed otherwise. After reading an article about Lady Paget, Sidney had hoped the death of his mother would be ruled as an accident, just as hers had. However, when her body was exhumed and autopsied by Sir Bernard Spilsbury, the tale took an interesting turn. After examining the body of Mrs. Fox it was determined she was strangled to death, because her lungs lacked the presence of soot and she had bruising on her pharynx.

As a result of the autopsy findings, police believed the story Sidney Harry Fox told was not accurate and felt he lied. The suspicion of police and investigators was further heightened after Fox claimed on the life insurance policies. On November 3, 1929, Sidney was charged with the murder of his mother and placed under arrest.

The Trial of Sidney Harry Fox

On March 12, 1930, the trial of Sidney Harry Fox began in Lewes, England. The prosecutors on the case were Sir William Jowitt and Sir Henry Curtis Bennett. Fox was represented in the matter by defense attorney J.D. Cassels. The prosecution contented Sidney had gotten Rosaline intoxicated and strangled her to death in order to inherit life insurance money.

Fox's defense attorney was not able to challenge the validity of the bruising on the pharynx, because by the time experts examined the body the marks were gone due to decomposition. The evidence against Fox was largely circumstantial, but powerful. Prosecuting attorney Sir William Jowitt subjected Sidney to grueling cross examination and the testimony he gave looked feeble at best. On the stand, Fox fell apart and his story quickly unraveled, making his guilt palpable.

The jury convicted Fox for the death of his mother and there were no grounds for an appeal. Sidney Harry Fox was later hanged to death at Maidstone prison on April 8, 1930. The case of Sidney Harry Fox is extremely unusual, because it is a rare example of matricide that is not at all common in the United Kingdom.

Jack Gilbert Graham

Introduction

John "Jack" Gilbert Graham was an American born mass-murderer who killed 44 people on a United Airlines Flight in 1955. Jack hated his mother Daisie King with a passion and he wanted nothing more than to be rid of her. He concocted an idea to plant dynamite in her luggage, which would leave him free to inherit part of her $150,000 estate after she died. Witnesses to the plane crash have varying stories, some saying it blew up in the air and others saying it exploded upon impact with the ground. In the end, many people lost their lives, and as for Jack Graham, he was found guilty of the bombing and sentenced to death.

Childhood

Jack Graham was born on January 23, 1932 in Denver, Colorado. At the age of three, Jack's father died suddenly and he was placed in an orphanage because his mother could not care for him. Jack lived in a long succession of foster homes until he was 13 years old. Daisie was married to a man named John Earl King in 1940, and after the marriage she brought Jack to live with them.

John and Daisie experienced financial problems, finding it hard to earn a living. John King began to sell off the large ranch the couple had bought an acre at a time. By 1950, after having completely sold off the entire ranch, the family moved to Yampa, Colorado. Daisie King was a very intelligent businesswoman and invested in a series of profitable drive-in restaurants.

The Teenage Years

In 1948, Jack Graham entered the U.S. Coast Guard. His service record was not impressive, and he received an honorable discharge a year later. During his time in the military, Graham went absent without leave for a total of 63-days. When he went back to Denver, he held several jobs, but did not do well at any of them.

By 1951, Jack Graham was employed as a clerk with a manufacturing company and he stole payroll checks that amounted to thousands of dollars. Jack forged the name of the company president on each check and with the proceeds he bought himself a new convertible. After purchasing the convertible, Jack Graham left for parts unknown and the police filed charges for his arrest.

What Strained Jack Gilbert Graham's Relationship with his Mother?

Jack Graham had a lengthy criminal record rife with theft, forgery and many other infractions. By 1955, he was married and had two children. Jack's family lived with his mother in a large home, which Daisie had paid for in East Denver. Soon, he was managing the drive-in restaurant and the business was thriving. However, just when things seemed to be looking up for the Graham family, relations between mother and son became strained.

Around early 1955, Jack had to pay his mother back for all the money she had spent on lawyers and bailing him out of jail. In addition to paying his mother back for all the money she spent keeping him out of jail, Jack also had to pay her rent for the house they shared. Graham publically fought with his mother, with most of the arguments being about money. It was at this time rumors began to circulate that Jack was stealing money from his family. By the end of 1955, Graham had nearly repaid the entire debt to his mother, but his anger and resentment festered under the surface.

What Happened to United Airlines Flight 629?

On November 1, 1955, 6:52 p.m. 44 people in Denver, Colorado boarded United Airlines

Flight 629 bound for Seattle, Washington. The flight came from New York's La Guardia Airport, making a stopover in Chicago before landing in Denver. Minutes after the plane took off from Denver; it exploded and killed everyone on board.

Flaming plane wreckage fell from the sky over tracts of farmland and landed in beet fields near Longmont, Colorado. Daisie King, Graham's mother was on the flight traveling to Alaska to visit with her daughter. After the Civil Aeronautics Board examined the plane wreckage, it became clear the aircraft itself had not exploded, but the source was something else entirely.

The Investigation of United Airlines Flight 629

The FBI investigated the scene and reported the passenger's luggage smelled like gunpowder or an exploding firecracker. Over a period of several weeks, search teams collected every scrap of wreckage they could find. Each location was recorded and every piece was meticulously cataloged. After careful investigation of all the evidence and wreckage, it was determined the explosion occurred near the luggage compartment of the airplane.

Part of investigating the plane crash included investigators looking at insurance claims on all of the passengers. It was discovered that many passengers had large life insurance policies that were purchased right before the flight. Six passengers had the maximum allowed at the time and agents checked over these purchases, recording the names of the beneficiaries.

Investigators working at the crash site were checking items recovered from the wreckage and agents took special notice of the items belonging to Daisie King. The property investigators recovered travelers checks, letters and newspaper clippings. The clippings had information about King's son, Jack who had been arrested in 1951, for forgery in Denver, Colorado.

Person of Interest

Upon further checking, agents found Daisie King carried a flight insurance policy for $37,500 and it named her son Jack, as the beneficiary. Upon her death, investigators also discovered he would inherit a large portion of the financial proceeds from her estate. After inquiring with local authorities, flight investigators learned of a suspicious explosion at Daisies' restaurant. An insurance claim was made on the restaurant and Jack Graham received a payout.

Jack Gilbert Graham had soon become a person of interest in the bombing of United Airlines Flight 629. Considering his troubled background and what he stood to inherit upon Daisies' death, the FBI decided to dig a bit more into the background of Jack Graham. After conducting a search of the Graham home, FBI agents found copper wire, which could be used in detonating primer caps and a separate $37,000 insurance policy on Daisie King, which named Jack as the sole beneficiary.

Graham was brought into police headquarters and subjected to days of relentless questioning. After some time, Graham relented and confessed what he had done. He described in great detail how he constructed and planted the bomb that took the life of his mother and forty-three other innocent people.

The Trial and Execution of Jack Gilbert Graham

The trial of Jack Gilbert Graham began in 1956 and it resulted in Colorado becoming the first state to allow television cameras into the courtroom. There was no federal statute outlining the crime or punishment for blowing up an airplane. However, based upon Graham's confession to the crime, the Colorado district attorney moved to try him for premeditated murder in the death of his mother, Daisie King.

On April 21, 1956, Graham entered the courtroom in downtown Denver and he did not know what to expect. Crime scene investigators, expert witnesses, technicians, scientists and other law enforcement personnel were called to the stand to give testimony that day. After all of the incriminating evidence was introduced to the court, along with Graham's 20-

page confession, it was almost an open and shut case.

Graham did not testify in his own defense, in fact he flatly refused to take the stand and requested his wife not testify on his behalf. The entire defense testimony lasted less than two hours and after deliberating for one hour and twelve minutes, the jury came back with a guilty verdict.

Jack Gilbert Graham was found guilty of first-degree murder and the conviction was an automatic death sentence. In February 1956, Graham attempted suicide in his prison cell and was placed under suicide watch. Anti-death penalty groups began to file appeals on his behalf, in an attempt to halt the execution. However, Graham was adamant about wanting to die and just get it over with.

Graham's execution was set for January 12, 1957 at 8:00 p.m. There were 12 witnesses who signed up to watch the event and dozens of reporters were outside the prison to record the day's events. Warden Harry Tinsley told reporters when he arrived at Graham's cell; he was in a jovial mood and good spirits, despite the execution closely looming.

Graham was stripped naked and given a pair of prison issue shorts. He removed his clothing and put the shorts on, walking quickly towards the execution chamber. The warden, three guards and a minister then escorted Jack into the gas chamber. Graham sat down in the metal chair and a black mask was put over his head.

After the warden and others exited the gas chamber, the room was filled with a poisonous cyanide fog. Jack gagged and wheezed; he let out an audible scream and within moments fell into unconsciousness. Jack Gilbert Graham was pronounced dead by prison doctors at 8:08 p.m. on January 11, 1957; his remains were removed and cremated.

The Legacy of Jack Gilbert Graham

Graham was an enigma in death, just as he had been in life. He never expressed any sorrow or remorse for the airplane bombing, nor did he ever explain his burning hate for his mother. Graham had a brief conversation with Warden Tinsley the evening of his execution during which he stated he never felt any remorse and was not sorry for what he had done.

CHARLES WHITMAN

Introduction

Charles Joseph Whitman was an American engineering student and former marine. He became known as the "Texas Bell Tower Sniper" after he climbed into the bell tower at the University of Texas and opened fired on the people below. Before the shooting, Whitman had killed his wife and mother. He then proceeded to the campus, climbed the bell tower with a rifle and fired on the crowds below for a total of 96-minutes. When the shooting was over, 16 people were killed and 32 others were left wounded. The shooting was the worst massacre on an American college campus, until the Virginia Tech tragedy in 2007.

Who was Charles Whitman?

Charles Joseph Whitman was born on June 24, 1941 in Lake Worth, Florida to Margaret and Charles "C.A." Whitman. C.A. Whitman was raised in an orphanage and was a self-made man who worked as a plumber. C.A. would accept no weakness in his sons and he ruled the household like a dictator with an iron fist. It was not uncommon for C.A. to beat his wife and children; he had a bad temper and was brutal with his discipline.

The Whitman family had the outward appearance of normalcy, while C.A.'s seething temper and high expectations meant life was anything but happy for his wife and children. The Whitmans drove the latest models of cars; the home was the nicest in the neighborhood and had all the amenities wealth could bring. However, underneath the picture of perfection, the luxurious lifestyle did nothing to quell the troubles brewing within the household.

Early Childhood

As a child, Charles Whitman was described as a polite and well-mannered child who rarely showed any display of temper. Charles was extremely intelligent and a gifted student, with an IQ revealed to be 139 when he was just 6-years old. The young Whitman also excelled at piano and became an Eagle Scout. His parents encouraged his academic achievements and failure in the Whitman family was unacceptable. If C.A. got even the slightest indication of non-compliance from his sons, he would use his fists, a belt or paddle as punishment.

Eagle Scout

C.A. Whitman collected firearms and he taught each of his boys from an early age how to shoot. He regularly took the boys on hunting trips; Charles came to love hunting and became an accomplished marksman. At the age of 11, Charles Whitman joined the Eagle Scouts and earned 21 merit badges within slightly over a year.

At 12 years old, Charles Whitman earned the rank of Eagle Scout and was reportedly the youngest person in the world to do so. Around the same time, Charles got an extensive newspaper job delivering the Miami Herald throughout his neighborhood. From the beginning Charles Whitman displayed all the traits of an overachieving hard-worker and never tried to raise the ire of his father.

The High School Years

In September of 1955, Charles Whitman entered St. Ann's High School in West Palm Beach, Florida. As a student, he was popular, intelligent and well liked by teachers and fellow students. By October, Charles had saved up enough money from his newspaper route to purchase a Harley Davidson motorcycle.

Whitman graduated in June of 1959; he was seventh in a class of seventy-two students. In June of 1959, a short time before Charles Whitman turned 18, the tension between him and his father reached a breaking point. Charles came home from a party intoxicated and C.A. was not happy. In reaction to his sons open defiance, C.A. beat Charles and threw him into the pool, where he nearly drowned. After the incident, Charles secretly went and enlisted into the U.S. Marines Corps, leaving for basic training on July 6, 1959.

The Military Years

It was very important for Charles Whitman to be the best marine he could be, an attitude largely due in part to having been programmed for perfection by his father. He was eager to prove himself as a man and he took every opportunity to advance that was presented to him. Charles spent the first part of his military career assigned to the Guantanamo Naval Base in Cuba.

He worked hard, followed directions and studied constantly for the many examinations he had to take. He earned a Good Conduct Medal, a Sharpshooter Badge and the Marine Corps Expeditionary Medal. As a shooter, he excelled at rapid fire from a long distance and he showed chilling accuracy with moving targets.

The Navy offered a special science education program and it greatly appealed to Charles Whitman. He studied hard, took a competitive examination and then appeared before a selection committee that picked him to be the candidate. He would have to earn a degree in engineering from a selected college and after that, he would need to complete Officer's Candidate School. His books and tuition would be paid for by the Corps, and in addition he would receive a monthly stipend of $250.00.

In September of 1961, Charles was accepted at the University of Texas in Austin. After years of leading a rigid and disciplined life, he was suddenly able to decide how he wished to spend his free time. Almost immediately after entering college, Charles began to get into trouble. He and some friends were arrested and charged with deer poaching and he amassed gambling large debts, which he refused to repay.

Charles married his girlfriend, Kathy Leissner in August of 1962, but the Marine Corps did not take his previous bad behavior lightly. The scholarship from the Navy was withdrawn and Charles was returned to active duty in February of 1963.

The Marines stationed Charles at Camp Lejeune in North Carolina. Having to return to discipline and structure was oppressive to him. Kathy remained in Texas to finish up her degree and Charles started to become very lonely. He tried to resume his scholarship, but failed and was told the time he spent in Austin did not count towards active duty reenlistment. Slowly, things in his life started to spiral and Charles became angry.

Charles began to resent the Marine Corps and it was reflected in his actions and defiant behavior. In November of 1963, he was court-martialed for gambling and having an unauthorized non-military issue pistol. He threatened a fellow soldier over an unpaid loan. He was arrested, found guilty and sentenced to 30-days confinement and 90-days of hard labor. All of these events were combining to make for the perfect storm.

The Events that Led Up to the University of Texas Shootings

Because of the incidents at Camp Lejeune, Charles was demoted from his rank of Lance Corporal to Private. In 1963, while he was waiting to be court-martialed, Whitman began to write in a diary. He wrote about his life in the Corps, his interactions with Kathy and other family members. Charles outlined his frustrations about the inefficiencies of the Marine Corps. When he wrote about Kathy, Charles praised her as a wife and wrote about missing her, vowing to never become abusive like his father.

Two close friends of Charles and Kathy spoke of how he had told them he struck Kathy three times throughout their marriage. Charles despised himself for being abusive and resolved to become a better husband. The greatest fear he carried was becoming violent and abusive like his father. Charles was determined to not become a monster.

In May of 1966, Margaret Whitman decided to divorce C.A. because of years of physical abuse. Charles drove to Florida to help her move and was so afraid of his father's violence, he asked police to come to the home as his mother packed her things. Margaret moved to Austin, secured work in a cafeteria and was able to move into her own apartment. Because of the ongoing stress he was under, Charles started to experience blinding headaches.

On the evening before the campus shootings, Charles wrote in his journal about his undying love for Kathy. Friends and family of Charles agreed he was under great strain and trying to do too much, but nobody noticed he was slowly and quietly being pushed toward violence. As the summer of 1966 wore on, Charles began to fantasize about killing.

The Murders of Kathy and Margaret Whitman

On July 31, 1966, Charles and Kathy Whitman visited with some close friends, leaving the apartment around 5:50 p.m. so Kathy could go to work. At approximately 6:40 p.m. Charles began to type his suicide letter. He requested an autopsy be performed on his body, to see if there were any biological reasons for his behavior and headaches.

Charles also wrote that he decided to kill his wife and mother in order to relieve them of the suffering in this world and protect them from embarrassment. He did not however mention anything about his decision to open fire on the University of Texas campus. Just after midnight, Charles drove to his mother's apartment; it is thought he rendered her unconscious and stabbed her in the heart.

After killing his mother, Charles drove back to the apartment he shared with Kathy and stabbed her in the heart three times while she was sleeping. He left notes next to the bodies of his mother and wife. He left instructions in the apartment requesting for two rolls of film to be developed and left personal letters for his two brothers.

The Bell Tower Shootings

On the morning of August 1, 1966, Charles cashed some worthless checks and began to collect his arsenal of weapons. He purchased a

Universal M1 carbine, two additional ammunition magazines and eight more boxes of ammunition from a hardware store. He then drove to Chuck's Gun Shop where he purchased six more boxes of ammunition, more carbine magazines, and gun cleaner. After leaving Chuck's, he drove to Sears where he bought a Sears model 12-gauge semiautomatic shotgun and then he went back home.

After taking stock of his arsenal at home, Charles packed up food, coffee, vitamins and other supplies. Shortly before heading to the bell tower, he changed his clothes, dressing in khaki coveralls over his jeans and t-shirt. At approximately 11:45, Whitman headed to the University of Texas campus.

He entered the bell tower with his munitions and other supplies, taking his place on the 27th floor. He began to open fire on the crowds below using the "one shot, one kill" sniper philosophy. He never shot twice at anyone who had fallen to the ground. Whitman shot at the crowds on campus for ninety-six full minutes, before police stormed the bell tower and shot him to death.

Aftermath

For many years after the shootings, the University of Texas kept the bell tower closed to the public. In October of 1998, university president Larry Faulkner announced plans to reopen the tower and asked for support from University Regents. On September 15, 1999 the tower was opened to the public again. The actions of Charles Whitman have been exorcised from the campus, but safety measures and heightened security remind visitors of how the events of the past can never be completely forgotten.

JOHN EMIL LIST

Introduction

John Emil List was an American-born mass murderer; he was convicted of murdering his mother, wife and children. He had planned the murder of his family with such precision; it took a month before anyone found the bodies. He was a long-time fugitive from justice and built a brand new life in the Denver, Colorado area. John List evaded justice for 18-years, until his story was chronicled on America's Most Wanted. After the episode aired, a neighbor recognized him and alerted local law enforcement.

List was arrested, found guilty of first-degree murder and sentenced to five terms of life imprisonment.

Early Life and Childhood

John Emil List was born in Bay City, Michigan on September 17, 1925. He was the only child of German-American parents, John and Alma List. The List family belonged to the German Lutheran Church, Missouri Synod. They lived in a grand Victorian home and John was relegated to sleeping in the parlor, with no privacy or personal space. He learned to be a quiet, tidy person and always put his things away neatly, so he could easily blend into the background.

John List, Sr. only dealt with his son through his wife and referred to him as "the boy." As a child, John was expected to behave appropriately, do well in school and uphold the Lutheran faith. He did not spend much time with his father growing up and his father apparently did not like children very much. Alma was overly protective of her son and brought him up in life focused on faith and the Lutheran Church.

Alma always harbored an abnormal fear John Jr. would get sick, so she watched over him constantly and kept his dressed warmly at all times. He was not allowed to have a normal childhood and could never go outside or play with other children in the neighborhood. Alma smothered John Jr. and left an impression on him that the world was a very cold, dangerous place.

High School Years

In high school List was a loner, and made few friends and had no girlfriends. After graduating, he had enough of his mother's smothering ways and his father's rejection. To find his place in the world, John enlisted in the Army in 1943. John's father passed away in 1944, and he went back home for the funeral. At the time, people noticed a distinct difference in his personality and noted he displayed no outward signs of grief over the death of his father.

After the funeral, John was shipped to the Pacific theater, but the war was mostly over and he never experienced much action. He came home and had obtained a fascination with firearms, particularly an Austrian Steyr pistol that would be used some 30-years later when he killed his own family.

The College Years

At the urging of his mother, John decided to take up accounting as a major in college. He attended the University of Michigan in Ann Arbor and graduated with degrees in business administration and accounting. Just as he was starting a new job, he was called back to the service to fight in the Korean War. Again, he entered towards the end of the conflict and never got a chance to see any action.

It was around this time that John met his future wife when he was stationed in Virginia. Helen Taylor was a recent military widow and had a nine year old daughter. John courted and romanced her, and she was eager to find a new husband. Alma did not approve of Helen, because she had had several miscarriages and was not a person of the Lutheran faith.

Marriage & Family

Helen later got pregnant and John knew he would have to marry her very soon. He seemed proud of the prospect of becoming a father and the couple was married on December 1, 1951. After the wedding, Alma always reminded her son he had married someone unworthy of him. It soon came out that Helen was not pregnant at all and soon she came to regret her decision to marry John so quickly.

Helen and Alma never got along and John was always in the middle of their spats and disagreements. Helen gave birth to the couple's first child Patricia in January of 1955 and Alma finally came to accept her daughter-in-law. John took a new job with a growing company and their son John Frederick was born. The future was shining bright for the List family, but the happy times were not to last.

Helen was never interested in the Lutheran faith and it left John with feelings of anger and resentment. Helen became pregnant again, which made her extremely unhappy and upset. After the couple's third child Frederick Michael was born in 1958, Helen turned to substance abuse.

The List marriage began to crumble as Helen drank, took pills and neglected the children. Much of the child rearing fell onto John's shoulders, but he rarely complained. During this time, the company John worked for merged and he lost his position. Helen grew to hate John and overspent the couple's money. He grew angry when she attracted the attention of other men, silently seething with hate and jealousy.

John lost his job at Xerox and Helen's health started to decline due to her substance abuse and previously undiagnosed syphilis. The couple's finances were in a shambles, but John finally landed a job in New Jersey. In order to fund the move to Westfield in 1965, John borrowed money from his mother for the down payment on a house. Alma agreed to the arrangement on the condition she came to live there with the family.

The new job only lasted for a year; John just did not have the social skills or sales experience to pull in new clients. He was fired and faced with the looming reality of a huge mortgage, high utility bills, family expenses, a bad marriage and an elderly, nagging mother. Alma signed power of attorney over her finances to John and she lost her entire life savings. Things began to spiral downhill and John felt enormous pressure with the situation he found himself in.

The Day of the Murders
On November 9, 1971, John Emil List systemically and methodically killed off his entire family. The first victim was Helen; she was shot in the jaw as she sat eating breakfast. While Helen lay dead on the kitchen floor, John went upstairs and entered his mother's apartment. He entered his mother's domicile without knocking and shot her point blank over the left eye.

List went and picked up his daughter Patty at school because she was ill. He got back to the house and quickly rushed inside before Patty, he then hid behind the front door. As Patty came through the door, he shot her at close range in the back of the head. Later in the afternoon he picked up Fred from his job, took him home and before the boy had even removed his coat, John shot him in the back of the head with a single bullet.

John Jr. was not due to come home until after soccer practice, so List prepared to leave as soon as he had killed the last of his children. John Jr. arrived home earlier than expected and when he came in the door he spotted his father pointing a gun at him. The two struggled and two shots went into the floor and one into the ceiling. After a violent fight to the death, John Sr. shot his son in the eye and shot him ten more times to ensure he was dead.

Fleeing the Scene

John List spent the night with the bodies of his family and the next morning he fled with $2500 in his pocket. John wound up settling in Boulder, Colorado around 1972 and he resumed working as an accountant under the name Robert Peter Clark. By 1975, John List, aka: Robert Clark, joined a Lutheran Church in Denver.

Soon after arriving in Denver, John met a woman and fell in love. He met Delores Miller at a singles social and the two began dating. Delores was impressed with his manners and gentle nature. When she asked him about his first wife, List told her she had died of cancer, but never showed her a picture. The two were married in 1985; it was not long afterward, Delores began to regret her decision.

The couple's marriage was rife with trouble and John went through a series of different jobs, never able to land something permanent. Delores and "Robert" spent the next several years moving around and living a less than happy life.

America's Most Wanted

In 1989, prosecutors from Union County approached the producers of the Fox TV show, America's Most Wanted. It was done in order to have the producers take a fresh look at the List case. To assist, the show's producers brought in a forensic sculptor and a criminal psychologist.

Through studying photographs of John List, the forensic sculptor was able to imagine how the man may have looked in 1989. He imagined John would still be wearing horn-rimmed glasses, to make himself seem successful. On May 21, 1989, Fox chronicled the story of John Emil List on an episode of America's Most Wanted and the show reached more than 22 million viewers.

A woman who lived in Richmond, Virginia believed the bust created by the forensic sculptor looked just like her neighbor Robert Clark. Clark was a devout Lutheran accountant who wore horn-rimmed glasses. FBI agents went to the home of "Robert Clark" and confronted Delores, who was stunned. "Robert Clark" was arrested on June 1, 1989 and fingerprints later confirmed he was actually John List.

Trial and Conviction

At his trial, John List admitted he was suffering anxiety due to the grave financial difficulties he faced in 1971. He had lost his job and kept it from his family by hiding at the local bus station every day. A court appointed psychiatrist testified List was suffering from obsessive-compulsive disorder and felt he had only two options; welfare or killing his family.

On April 12, 1990, John Emil List was convicted of five counts of first-degree murder and sentenced to five consecutive terms of life imprisonment. He spent his years in prison content with what he had done and felt oddly confident his family would forgive him for his actions in the afterlife.

John List died on March 21, 2008 from complications due to pneumonia. No family members stepped forward to claim his body and he was buried next to his mother in Frankenmuth, Michigan.

ANTONY BAEKELAND

Introduction

Brooks Baekeland was wealthy, handsome and intelligent; he was the heir to the Bakelite plastic fortune. Barbara Daly, a model, was once hailed as one of New York's ten most beautiful girls. Barbara and Brooks were married after a whirlwind courtship, but the marriage was based upon deception from the start. The couple had one child, Antony. Brooks never took notice of his son, whereas to Barbara he was the most perfect child ever born. Tony and Barbara had a troubled relationship because she could never quite get past his homosexual lifestyle. After years of an abusive and troubled relationship with his mother, Antony stabbed Barbara to death with a kitchen knife on November 17, 1972, at her London home.

Brooks and Barbara Baekeland: The Marriage

After falsely claiming she was pregnant, Barbara Daly and Brooks Baekeland were married in a quickie service in California. Once married, the couple set up house in the Upper East Side of New York; living in a luxurious apartment. Brooks and Barbara led an opulent lifestyle, hosting parties that were attended by such notables as Greta Garbo, Yasmin Aga Khan and Tennessee Williams. It was at these parties Barbara became known for being mentally unstable, due to her random, irrational outbursts, coupled with bouts of crippling depression.

The couple welcomed a son Antony on August 28, 1946; for a time it seemed the family settled into a short period of domestic bliss. However, from the summer of 1954 onward the couple began to lead a mostly nomadic lifestyle, jetting between London, Paris and Italy. Throughout the 1960's, the family mostly lived in Paris where Brooks met a woman who was fifteen years younger than him.

The couple began to have marital issues after Brooks started having an affair with the younger woman. He asked Barbara for a divorce, she tried to commit suicide and he ended the affair. In 1967, the family moved to Switzerland and lived at the Cadaques, a Spanish resort. It was while living in Switzerland that the lives of the family were forever changed.

Homosexual Lifestyle

While living with his parents in Switzerland, Antony was introduced to a homosexual Australian named Jake Cooper. Known for having dashing good looks and a silver tongue, Jake Cooper was anything but a good influence on Tony. Cooper was referred to as "Black Jake"; he lived in an abandoned farmhouse with an entourage of hippies who were into drugs and practiced black magic.

Tony fell hard for the Australian, trying desperately to secure his love by lavishing him with expensive gifts and giving him money. Cooper was a bad influence and introduced Antony to hallucinogenic drugs. The hold Jake Cooper exacted over Tony was witnessed by a friend of the family, who quickly reported what was going on to Barbara who was away vacationing in Switzerland at the time.

When Barbara learned about the homosexual affair, she traveled to Spain to bring Antony back home with her to Switzerland. However, upon reaching the border to France, Antony was discovered as not having a passport. After a confrontation with border patrol, the pair was arrested and jailed.

Barbara Baekeland was determined to rid Jake from Tony's life; she would stop at nothing to do it. While Tony was in love with Jake, it was also during this time he began seeing a French girl named Sylvie. Barbara was thrilled Tony finally had a girlfriend; she invited the young girl over for dinner and immediately started talking about the couple getting married.

Barbara's husband Brooks was also seeing Sylvie, but it was not discovered until the following February. When she found out about the affair, Barbara attempted to commit suicide again through taking an overdose of sedatives mixed with copious amounts of vodka. Brooks did not return to Barbara as he had done many times before. Sylvie also attempted suicide through an overdose, possibly in a plea for attention. Brooks eventually choose Sylvie, telling Barbara he wanted a divorce in no uncertain terms.

Barbara and Antony: The Beginning of the End

After Brooks left her, Barbara began experiencing a downward spiral; her mental stability was questionable at best. She began having bizarre thoughts about how she could "cure" Tony of his homosexuality, convinced she could turn him around if she were to seduce him.

Barbara and Tony spent the summer of 1969 living in a house lent to them by an Austrian archduke. Fueled by drinking and smoking marijuana in a villa with no phone or electricity, the relationship between mother and son took a fateful turn. In a drunken and drug fueled haze, Barbara Baekeland successfully seduced her son Antony, feeling it was the right thing to do.

She was very honest about the fact she had sexual relations with her son, even bragging about it to her friends and others. The damage to Tony's psyche was done, the results of which would prove to be catastrophic. Later that summer, Brooks came to Majorca to vacation with Sylvie, not knowing his wife and son were there.

When Barbara found out about Brooks and Sylvie being in Majorca, Tony started to visit them and his mental health was further damaged. He begged his father to return to his mother, leaving pleading notes for him everywhere. Witnesses to the events described Tony as having the mental state of a small child. Tony became violent, breaking a typewriter and many other objects in the home. Brooks angrily threw Antony out of the house, cutting off all contact with his son out of frustration.

Barbara took no notice of how fragile her son was, as she routinely ignored his outbursts of inappropriate behavior. The following summer Barbara retuned to New York, and not long afterward Tony followed. Tony's behavior took on a more sinister tone once he enrolled in a New York Art School. He became withdrawn and solemn, and would not respond to anyone. It appeared he was lost in a catatonic state. Barbara could no longer ignore the mental issues her son was facing, particularly after he turned up at home one evening delusional, which frightened her greatly.

The Warning Signs Everyone Ignored
Barbara came to be extremely fearful of her son's erratic behavior, quietly arranging for Tony to be admitted to a private psychiatric facility. However, he was discharged after only six weeks because Barbara could not afford to continue paying for treatment. Once released, Tony quickly relapsed; one night he beat his mother unconscious with a heavy wood walking stick.

After the beating episode, Tony was diagnosed with having schizophrenia and it was recommended he be returned to the mental hospital. However, Brooks refused to pay for Tony to be admitted to the mental facility because he felt psychiatrists were worthless. Tony was once again released and went to live with his mother, where his behavior quickly escalated. He became violent towards Barbara in front of horrified dinner guests, dragging her from her chair by the hair and beating her mercilessly.

In the final months of her life, Barbara experienced Tony's violent and unpredictable behavior on numerous occasions. During a fight between the two, he attempted to blind her by sticking her in the eye with an ink pen. Another time, Barbara was escorted home from dinner by a journalist; Tony appeared at the front door naked, brandishing a large knife as he ranted about killing his mother.

By the summer of 1972, Tony began to go into catatonic trances, clutching himself while rocking back and forth. Barbara arranged for him to see a psychiatrist recommended by a friend. The psychiatrist confirmed Tony was suffering from extreme schizophrenia, the situation was made all the worse by him not taking his medications. The doctor was concerned about Barbara's safety and was convinced Tony would harm her, but she did not pay any attention to the warning.

The Day of the Murder
Eighteen days after being cautioned about her son's violent tendencies and dismissing the warning, Barbara Baekeland was dead. On the morning of November 17, 1972, at her London penthouse, Tony Baekeland stabbed his mother to death with a kitchen knife to the heart. When the police arrived, he was calmly on the phone ordering Chinese takeout, appearing not to have a care in the world.

Life after Barbara Baekeland's Murder
Tony was judged mentally incapacitated and placed in a mental institution at the Broadmoor Hospital; he was released on July 21, 1980. He was freed on the provision that upon returning

to the states, he would reside in a halfway house so he could properly reintegrate back into society. Tony's father refused to have anything to do with the situation; he again wanted no contact with his son.

After flying from London to New York City, Antony went to stay with his 87-year old grandmother Nina Daly. Six days later, he stabbed her eight times in total, breaking several of her bones. He was arrested by the New York City Police Department and charged with attempted murder. Tony was sent to Riker's Island, the state's main prison.

On March 20, 1981, after being taken to court for an appearance, Tony found out his trial would not be held for another month. He had hoped to be granted a provisional bail, but the application from his defense lawyer was refused. A little more than an hour after returning to his cell, Tony was found dead at 3:30 p.m., having committed suicide by suffocating himself with a plastic bag.

Brooks Baekeland believed his son had been murdered, but others were convinced it was a suicide. The most ironic part of Tony's death was the instrument he used to take his own life. The plastic bag Tony Baekeland used to suffocate himself was made from the same material that brought his family immense wealth, but also heartbreaking tragedy.

BRETT REIDER

Introduction

　　Brett Reider is an American born killer who gained national attention when he stabbed his mother to death. At the age of 15-years old, he had suffered many years of abuse, which caused him to experience a mental breakdown. Brett's mother Claudia demanded perfection and would accept nothing less from her children. When Brett or his sister Alissa would disappoint her, she would fly into an uncontrollable rage, becoming abusive. Darwin Reider would not intervene between his wife and children, unless the situation became completely out of control. Because Darwin travelled extensively for work, it meant Brett was left alone to bear the brunt of his mother's rage.

Family Life

Brett Reider was born on October 8, 1977, the second child of Darwin and Claudia Reider. To those observing from the outside, the Reider family appeared to be picture perfect. Darwin was known for being a hard worker, while Claudia was heavily involved in charity work. The family appeared to have it all, but the façade was not meant to last.

As time passed, Claudia became obsessed with maintaining a pristine family image. She wanted her children to be nothing but the best at everything they did. She encouraged Brett and Alissa to become involved in sports and take advanced classes at school. The relentless drive for perfection soon led Claudia to become physically and emotionally abusive.

When her children did not measure up to her idea of perfection, Claudia would react with a barrage of physical abuse and verbal intimidation. Darwin Reider would not intervene in these disputes, unless he witnessed Claudia becoming physically violent with the children. However, he was away from home much of the time due to job responsibilities, so there were many things he did not see.

Darwin would call periodically to check in, telling Claudia he was working late, when in actuality he was living in hotels and doing anything possible to avoid going home. Meanwhile, Brett and Alissa were left alone to defend themselves against a violent and unstable mother. After the murder, Darwin was later blamed for not doing more; there were those who felt the situation could have been prevented had he been more proactive.

The Abuse of Claudia Reider

The abuse Claudia Reider was inflicting on her children was a well-kept family secret. Darwin and Claudia balanced high-powered professional careers and excelled at work. The couple had a beautiful home, were active in the community and both were devoted churchgoers. Home videos show the typical, All-American family, but Claudia's shouts of verbal abuse can be heard ringing loudly in the background.

It has been speculated that Claudia might have been suffering from untreated manic depression in the months leading up to her death. According to people who knew her, Claudia suffered from violent mood swings and erratic behavior, but at work she maintained a picture of the consummate professional. The constant mood swings and unstable behavior patterns were just a small portion of the problems she was dealing with in her life.

The Day of the Murder

On February 18, 1993, something in the Reider family went terribly wrong. Brett arrived at the family home around 4:30 p.m. and began to help Claudia unload groceries from the car. The two got into a violent argument over a

"B+" grade Brett had scored on a math test that day. Brett Reider went upstairs to his bedroom retrieving a hidden stun gun. He crept up behind his mother as she carried groceries into the house, fired the stun gun and she fell to the ground.

While Claudia was on the floor, Brett went to the kitchen and grabbed a butcher knife. He began to chase her around the home with the knife, poking her with it as they fought. When he had clear aim, Brett stabbed Claudia in the upper chest near her throat. The butcher knife severed her aorta; Claudia bled to death within a matter of minutes. Brett fled the family home; he ran to a neighboring home where rescue workers were called.

Nobody could say if what happened was a tragedy or a crime, but the fact remained; Claudia Reider was dead and the details surrounding the event were in dispute. To Darwin Reider, the event was a tragedy, following horrible mistakes made by two of the people he loved most in the world. He hired a defense attorney, posted bail and Brett was released into his custody.

The Trial

According to his defense attorney, Brett Reider chased his mother around the house with a butcher knife, but he did not intend to kill her. However, Claudia supposedly turned the tables on her son; she grabbed the knife and Brett knew he was in serious trouble. He was extremely frightened because he was very familiar with the look Claudia bore right before she would unmercifully batter him and his sister.

At the trial, Brett's defense attorney remarked in his opening statement that even though he had previously thought about killing his mother, it did not mean it was premeditated. However, the prosecuting attorney Greg Abboud had an entirely different concept. Abboud portrayed the killing as a carefully choreographed event, which was executed according to a premeditated plan.

Brett Reider had allegedly talked to friends about killing his mother, explaining in detail exactly how he would do it. He made friends at school with a boy who had access to firearms; the two would discuss various ways to kill Claudia. The prosecutor said Brett's actions the day of the murder matched everything he said and described to his friends.

Psychologist reports released in court show Brett was extremely polite and emotionally guarded, but not withdrawn. He earned A's and B's throughout school, got along well with his peers and exceled in football. However, no matter how well he would do, Brett was constantly obsessed with doing better. Brett's school counselor revealed through her conversations with him that he was under stress at home. He and his sister were dealing with abuse that had culminated over many years.

In the weeks before the shooting, there were ongoing conflicts between Brett and Claudia. The fights led to Brett being slapped around and having his hair pulled by his mother. However, the prosecuting attorney stopped short of stating he was actually abused. Brett was rebelling against his mother, with the two clashing about school, grades, his friends and girls.

Apparently a week before the stabbing Brett and his mother had another altercation. He had reportedly run away from home, staying out the entire night. Claudia again tried to clamp down on her son's defiant behavior, but it backfired. At the end of another screaming match, Brett ended up calling 9-1-1, this time he was threatening to kill himself.

Brett's defense attorney explained the plans to murder Claudia were nothing more than fantasies, stating even his friends knew the truth. He stated Brett never struck his mother or spoke back to her when she was calling him names and battering him. At the time of the stabbing, Claudia had started hitting him on the neck and back of the head; Brett could not take it anymore. Years of abuse, belittling and name-calling had caused him to erupt, and the resulting tempest was deadly.

On Thursday, August 26, 1993, a judge found Brett Reider guilty of second-degree murder for stabbing his mother to death. Before handing down the sentence, the judge verbally chastised Darwin Reider for standing by and doing nothing, while Claudia systematically abused the children. Prosecutors had asked for a first-degree murder conviction. However, the judge ruled for second-degree murder, because of the mental instability Brett was experiencing in the time before the murder.

Aftermath

Brett Reider entered the Nebraska Correctional Institute to begin serving his sentence on October 1, 1993. He received a sentence of 10-15 years for the second-degree murder of his mother. Brett was released from prison on July 16, 1999, while he was formally discharged from parole on March 7, 2003.

The Menendez Brothers

Introduction

The Menendez Brothers are best known for killing their wealthy parents Jose and Mary "Kitty" Menendez with a shotgun. Lyle and Erik grew up in Princeton, New Jersey and from an early age both boys were privileged, never knowing what it meant to work for something. Jose was a proud father who was dedicated to raising his boys to be successful in life. Lyle and Erik were raised in a rigid household where there were rules for everything. All of the expectations to be perfect became too much for the brothers; they believed the only way out was to murder their parents.

Jose and Kitty Menendez were married in 1961, secretly eloping due to family disapproval on both sides. The couple welcomed their first son, Joseph Lyle, on January 10, 1968; second son Erik was born on November 27, 1971. Although the beginning of the couple's marriage started as a partnership, soon Jose took over, controlling everything that happened within the family. The couple appeared to be living the American dream, but soon it was to come crashing down.

Childhood

Because Jose had fought and struggled to reach his dreams, he did not want to see his children have to do the same. He groomed Lyle and Erik to follow in his footsteps from the very start. Jose had rules for everything: what the boys could eat or read, the friends they could hang out with, right down to what they thought. The pressures of trying to meet the unrealistic expectations of an abusive father appeared early in the lives of Lyle and Erik.

The stress of living with a domineering father took its toll and manifested in a variety of ways. Both children developed stutters, stomach pains and had a habit of teeth grinding. Never were the effects of Jose's abuse more obvious than when people observed the temperaments of Lyle and Erik. Both boys were narcissistic and had volatile, hair-trigger tempers.

When the boy's got older, they were drawn together for companionship and bonded strongly in order to protect one another from Jose's abuse. Erik often told his friends of how he looked up to his older brother Lyle. Erik's friends could not understand the hero worship he exhibited towards Lyle, because to them it was clear he was nothing but trouble.

The boys' friends would often comment about how close Erik and Lyle were, but how different they were in personality. Erik was sensitive and quiet. Lyle was aloof and intelligent; he was described as having the stronger personality of the two brothers.

Throughout the summer of 1988, the Menendez brothers spent time in and out of trouble for various things. Erik and Lyle started breaking into houses around Calabasas. The brothers stole large amounts of cash and jewelry. They had found an easy way to get money and it did not involve asking their father or listening to his lectures about the value hard work.

The boys were caught and prosecuted for the burglaries. Jose was furious and did not want his sons to spend any time in jail. He hired a well-known defense attorney to represent them in court. The boys were given a plea agreement, but it involved Erik taking all responsibility for the burglaries, while Lyle was got off scot-free. Jose wrote a check to the victims for restitution; life went right back to the way it was before.

Summer of 1989

By the summer of 1989, Jose was doing well at his job and the company invested in a life insurance policy for $15 million. The company also purchased a policy in the same amount for Jose's family. Kitty was named as a beneficiary on the policy, which was typical under the California Community property laws.

Lyle began to experience trouble that summer. His girlfriend Christy informed him she was pregnant. Jose went to see her once he found out about the information. According to Lyle, his father intimidated Christy into having an abortion, while Kitty told people Jose had paid the girl off for $100,000. After the pregnancy scare was dealt with, Lyle was forbidden to see her again.

Lyle had been attending Princeton University after having been accepted in 1987. By the summer of 1989, his grades were slipping and he was placed on academic probation. Jose tried to reign in his expectations for Lyle and did not try to put his son under too much pressure. Additionally, Lyle was placed on disciplinary probation for damaging school property.

Erik had graduated from Beverly Hills High School and competed in a number of tennis tournaments that summer. He played well, winning some matches, but losing some too. When Erik returned home in August, he waited to start college at UCLA. He had been accepted to Berkeley, but chose to go to UCLA because it offered a better tennis program.

As the summer ended, there were tensions in the household. Kitty started locking her bedroom door at night and sleeping with rifles. She feared her sons were sociopaths, having told her therapist as much. She was afraid of her own children, not knowing what the boys were capable of doing.

The Murder

At 11:47 p.m. on August 20, 1989, Lyle made a phone call to 911, which was routed to the Beverly Hills police department. The call lasted for two and a half minutes; Lyle told the dispatcher his parents had been shot and killed. The Beverly Hills police arrived and found a chaotic scene.

When police approached the scene, Erik was running around hysterically screaming and crying. Lyle was trying to calm him down. It appeared to police from examining the crime scene that Jose and Kitty knew their attackers. No signs of forced entry were found and nothing was missing, which eliminated robbery as a motive for the shootings.

Police escorted Lyle and Erik to the station for questioning, even though at the time they were not considered suspects. During questioning, Erik became emotionally distraught. He started to cry uncontrollably, not being able to sit still or calm down. Lyle was collected, remaining in control and answering questions methodically. Because Lyle and Erik were not considered suspects in the shooting of their parents, police did not administer gunshot residue tests.

The Funeral

Lyle and Erik staged an elaborate funeral for Jose and Kitty on August 25, 1989. The boys arrived an hour late; Erik looked very uncomfortable, while Lyle appeared calm and collected. On August 28, 1998 a private funeral service was held at the university chapel at Princeton University.

Four days after the murders, Lyle and Erik began to go on expensive shopping sprees. The boys spent money lavishly, with the sprees being paid for by the proceeds from Jose's personal life insurance policy. There were new cars, designer clothes, jewelry, Rolex watches and gold money clips.

When everything was tallied up from Jose and Kitty's life insurance policies, property and other assets, the estate was valued at $14 million. Lyle and Erik would each inherit approximately $2 million apiece after everything was settled.

Investigators watched how the brothers carelessly threw money around and it aroused suspicion. By the end of 1989, Lyle and Erik had spent more than $1 million; police now considered they could be suspects in the killing of their parents.

Investigation

Erik confessed to his psychologist that he and Lyle had killed their parents. Lyle threatened the man and he then contacted the police. Lyle was arrested on March 8, 1990 near the mansion, after investigators received a tip he was planning to flee from the state. Erik was in Israel at the time his brother was arrested, but he came home three days later and turned himself in to the police.

The Trial

The Menendez brothers and the murder of Kitty and Lyle made headlines all over the world. Court TV broadcasted the trial during 1993. Defense attorney Leslie Abramson painted an elaborate picture, alleging the brothers had been driven to kill their parents because of suffering a lifetime of abuse.

Kitty Menendez was portrayed as being mentally unstable, selfish woman, who was addicted to drugs. Jose was described as an overbearing, egomaniac who relentlessly mentally and emotionally abused his sons. The first trial ended with a deadlocked jury.

The Los Angeles District Attorney Gil Garcetti immediately announced the brothers would be retried. The second trial was less publicized, because the judge did not allow television cameras into the courtroom.

At the retrial, both Lyle and Erik were convicted of two counts each of first-degree murder and conspiracy to commit murder. During the penalty phase of the trial, the jury did not support the death penalty, but recommended life imprisonment. On July 26, 1996, Lyle and Erik Menendez were sentenced to life imprisonment, with neither brother having a chance for parole.

AARON BROWN

Introduction

Aaron Brown, a resident of Bend, Indiana became famous when he killed his mother and stepfather. According to witnesses, Aaron and his mother Elizabeth were not on the best of terms since she married and he was less than happy about his stepfather Jeffery Grueb. However, there was no abuse documented within the family and nobody suspected Aaron was going to do what he did. On February 6, 1994, while his parents were out at a party, Aaron hid in the home and when they walked in the door, he shot them both in cold blood.

Childhood

Aaron Brown was born on August 2, 1977, to Elizabeth Harrison Grueb. She and Aaron's biological father never married; he disappeared from the picture before he was even born. Although Elizabeth was a single mother, it is reported during the early years of Aaron's childhood, she doted on her only child. At some point, perhaps the strain of single parenting may have become too much, because she reportedly began an odyssey into alcoholism.

Aaron Brown's later years were spent growing up with a mother who regularly abused alcohol, but it was never clear if she was physically or verbally abusive to him. Throughout his teens, Brown had a significant history of psychiatric referrals and diagnoses due to his behavioral issues. Aaron Brown was diagnosed with bipolar disorder and placed on medication to control the symptoms of his depression.

Jeffery Grueb was known to be physically and verbally abuse towards his stepson. Aaron grew up never knowing the true identity of his biological father; it was said to have haunted him throughout his childhood. When his mother married Jeffrey Grueb, everything in the household changed. Aaron was used to being ignored by his mother, but now he was subject to the insults, threats, physical and emotional abuse of her new husband.

Amazingly, unlike most other children who commit the crime of matricide, Aaron Brown did not have any prior record of delinquent behavior or a criminal record. It is thought with all of the emotional stress and abuse occurring in the household, Aaron became unable to handle it any longer. At some point, in the days leading up to February 6, 1994, he began to plan shooting his mother and stepfather; he openly admitted as much under police questioning.

The Day of the Shootings

February 6, 1994 passed like any other day. It was a Monday and Aaron left for high school, like he had done many times before. Elizabeth and Jeffrey Grueb had made plans to attend a family party that evening, leaving Aaron a note to remind him they would be gone when he got home. Aaron did the typical teenage activities, played video games, watched his favorite shows and went to visit with friends. However, something happened that night which would change everything.

According to court documents, in the early morning hours of February 6, 1994, Aaron Brown lay in wait for his mother and stepfather to return home from the party. Once the couple arrived home, they had barely made it inside the house when Aaron came out from his hiding spot and murdered them with a shotgun. A short time later, 16-year old Aaron Brown turned himself into the authorities.

Questioning by the Police

After Aaron turned himself into the police, they began to interrogate him about the events leading up to the shooting of his mother and stepfather. Aaron was a minor at the time of police questioning. He willingly confessed to killing his mother and stepfather, but could give no motive for the shootings.

Aaron Brown was arrested; charged with two counts of first-degree murder in the shooting deaths of Elizabeth and Jeffrey Grueb. There was to be no trial, with Aaron and his defense attorney working out a plea agreement with prosecutors. After a lengthy sentencing hearing held December 16, 1994, the court ordered him to serve fifty years on each count of murder, with the time to run consecutively.

Aaron Brown vs. State of Indiana Appeal: December 29, 1995

On December 29, 1995, Aaron Brown officially appealed his 100-year prison sentence. The appeal was overseen by Judge Riley. Public defenders Susan K. Carpenter and Lorraine

L. Rodts represented Brown in the case. Attorney General Pamela Carter and Deputy Attorney General Randi F. Elfenbaum represented the state of Indiana in the matter.

The basis for the appeal was grounded in two separated issues. The first matter was whether or not Brown had been deprived of the privilege of self-incrimination. He felt the court using his unwarranted statements made during his presentencing interview was unjust. Brown did not agree to the statements being used as a basis for imposing an unfair, consecutive sentence.

The second matter of the appeal concerned whether Aaron Brown's sentence of 100-years was unfair. Given light of the considerable mitigating circumstances presented at court during the sentencing hearing on December 16, 1994, his defense attorney argued it was not.

Brown contends he was deprived of his right against self-incrimination when the court used his statements from the presentencing report. Specifically, he was averse to the court considering a statement he made when asked a question by the presentencing investigator.

When asked if he would ever kill again, Brown answered yes, under certain unspecified circumstances he would. Aaron Brown also made other statements regarding he had no remorse for the murders, expressing no sorrow for what he had done.

Aaron Brown felt he was not properly given his Miranda rights during arrest, specifically never being advised of his right to remain silent before the presentence interview. The court rejected the argument, stating Brown should have known that any information obtained during a presentencing interview might be used to make a sentencing determination. The court felt there was no violation; Brown's rights were not impinged through the use of information that he provided on a voluntary basis.

In the next issue, the appeal states Brown felt his sentence was manifestly unreasonable, especially in light of the mitigating circumstances presented at trial. Brown committed his crimes in February 1994 and the sentencing was imposed according to the statutes of 1993. The statute states a person who commits murder shall be imprisoned for a fixed term of forty years, with not more than twenty years for aggravating circumstances.

Aaron Brown was given an enhanced sentence of fifty years imprisonment for each count of murder. The sentences were ordered to be served consecutively, which brings the total sentence to 100 years.

The decision to increase or decrease Brown's prison sentence was left up to the court. When a court exercises its discretion to amend a prison sentence, many things are taken into consideration. In the case of Brown's appeal, the court viewed the aggravated circumstances surrounding the case, ruling in support of imposing the original sentence.

Both of the appeal matters considered by the court were denied. Aaron Brown's appeal was unsuccessful because the court found he had and still has ties with a prison gang called the CPT, an acronym for Compton, California, an area known for gangs and violence. He still does not exhibit any remorse for killing his stepfather Jeffrey Grueb. As part of the pre-screening interview, Brown admitted he would kill again given the right set of circumstances.

The court feels Aaron Brown remains as much of a danger today as he was in 1994.

Where is Aaron Brown Today?

Aaron Brown's story was chronicled on an episode of "Lock up: Raw," on September 24, 2010. An interviewer visited with Brown and several other inmates at the Indiana Department of Corrections. Today, Aaron Brown is working with animals at the prison in a no-kill shelter program set up in 2002. He is slowly trying to make sense of what he did, to understand why his life has turned out the way it has.

When asked about the night of February 6,1994, Brown stated he wished he had a good reason for doing what he did, but he could not justify taking the life of his mother and stepfather. Aaron Brown is currently serving his 100-year prison sentence at the Indiana Department of Corrections. He will not be eligible for release from prison until February 29, 2040.

Dr. Idella Kathleen Hagen

Introduction

Dr. Idella Kathleen Hagen is a former physician who became famous after she murdered her elderly parents. Educated at Harvard and Rutgers, Idella graduated and embarked on a prestigious medical career. Dr. Hagen was the classic picture of success, working hard to achieve her goals. In August of 2000, Dr. Hagen was arrested and was charged with the suffocation death of her parents Idella and

James Hagen. At the time of the murder, she had moved back into her childhood home in order to take care of her frail parents. The police do not believe the killing was as an act of mercy, but are still unsure of what it was that led Dr. Hagen to kill.

Childhood and Early Life

Idella Kathleen Hagen was born on November 15, 1945, the only child of Idella and James Hagen. Dr. Hagen grew up in Chatham Township, New Jersey. Her father James was an optician and through his work, her interest in the medical field was piqued.

In high school, she got a summer job working with a doctor, further fueling her love for the medical field. Idella graduated from Chatham High School in 1963; her yearbook summaries include many classmates mentioning her sweetness. Her biography disclosed she was a modeling school graduate, with dreams of owning a bright, green Chevrolet Impala.

Breaking the Glass Ceiling

Idella Hagen went on from high school to attend Douglass College at Rutgers, and it was here she met Peter A. Cook. He was a graduate of Rutgers from Bedfordshire, England. The couple was married in 1969, following a quick courtship. After Peter and Idella were married, their life together was hectic due to the demands that came from her being in medical school.

In 1973, Idella graduated from Harvard Medical School. Soon after, she became the very first woman to be appointed as a urology resident at Massachusetts General Hospital. In 1982 she became chief of the urology division at Rutgers Medical School. Idella and Peter were divorced in 1979. The couple had no children.

In 1983, Idella was at a dance club at the Jersey Shore where she met William Tyrrell, an industrial engineer. William worked at Motion Systems, a company that made small industrial components. The couple was married in 1984. It was the second marriage for both of them and he brought with him two sons from his previous wife.

Dr. Hagen was a female working in a field of medicine predominantly filled with men. She grew disillusioned with the direction medicine was taking and the new money-conscious standards of medical care. William stated she would talk about how doctors were being driven out of medicine; she felt there were too many people involved in making medical decisions who did not need to be. Idella felt she had no freedom as a doctor because she had many restrictions due to health insurance companies.

Making Some Changes

By 1986, William stated she was feeling the strain of her profession and started to suffer from severe depression. The depression caused Idella to be hospitalized for many weeks; it was believed she suffered from bipolar disorder. Idella was put on medication to control the symptoms of her depression and she quickly resumed her work with little to no disruptions.

Around the time Idella was diagnosed with bipolar disorder, she and William began talking about making some new changes in their life. The couple had recently vacationed in St. Thomas and the Virgin Islands. They loved the islands so much they constructed a vacation home and thought about relocating to open a business.

In 1987, the couple discovered the Villa Olga, a small hotel and restaurant in St. Thomas. The property had once been the home of the Russian consulate. William and Idella fell in love with the quaint hotel and surrounding property, taking out a lease for $600,000.

Idella cut back her work at the medical school to part-time hours and the pair moved to St. Thomas. The hotel was renamed the West Indies Inn; soon renovations were underway. The hotel was enlarged from eight rooms to nineteen. For a while, it seemed Idella and William were doing well, but the hand of fate would soon intervene and the good times would end.

Hurricane Hugo came roaring through in 1989, and it ravaged the entire island and left the inn with major damage. However, Idella and William remained optimistic, deciding to repair the property. The next strike was the Persian Gulf War and unstable stock market, which made it unaffordable for people to travel. Airlines began to founder, making it difficult for travelers to get flights to the islands. Disappointed and frustrated, Idella and William gave up their dreams.

Life Back in the United States

In 1992, William retuned to the United States and went back to work as an operations manager for Motion Systems. Idella remained in St. Thomas, trying to sell the lease on the property. She remained on the island for about a year, until the original seller took the property back again. The couple wound up losing about $250,000 in the end.

They decided to keep the vacation home in St. Thomas, while resuming their lives in New Jersey. William and Idella purchased a clapboard home on the Shrewsbury River in Rumson, New Jersey. Dr. Hagen started unpaid medical research at Robert Wood Johnson where rats were being used to find a treatment for bladder cancer.

The Marriage Unravels

In the subsequent years after leaving St. Thomas, William and Idella started to experience marital issues. They were both stubborn people. She stopped practicing medicine because it was not fulfilling for her any longer. When Idella stopped achieving goals, she was not happy, which in turn made the lives of everyone around her miserable.

The event that broke the marriage down irretrievably happened in 1995. William climbed on his motorcycle to take a ride with the intent of going to visit with a friend. He stopped at a stop sign and then proceeded to drive on. William had limited vision in his left eye because of a childhood accident. He did not see the car coming from his left and it hit his motorcycle.

The impact left William with broken ribs and a mangled left leg.

Doctors told him the prognosis; amputate the leg or face years of surgery trying fix it, with no guarantee it would ever be 100%. William wanted to just have the leg removed and get on with life, but Dr. Hagen was adamant he keep the leg. He decided to have his leg removed, coming to the conclusion his marriage was over. He never went back home upon leaving the hospital and checked into a motel.

It took a year to reach a divorce agreement, due to finances and a prenuptial agreement. In August 1997, Dr. Idella Kathleen Hagen was a newly divorced woman worth a little more than $1 million. She shuttled back and forth between the vacation home in St. Thomas and her parents' residence in Chatham Township. She quit doing research and lived in a basement apartment in her childhood home.

At the time of the divorce, Idella seemed to struggle with her sense of self-identity. Everything she had accomplished for herself seemed to melt away. She had no husband, no career, no children and no foreseeable future. Idella began to worry about money; though she seemed frugal, financial security was very important to her.

She had real estate agents in St. Thomas put her vacation home for sale on June 22, 1998, but it was promptly removed from the market a few weeks later. She spoke to a former colleague expressing concerns about the expenses related to taking care of her parents, but she had not liquidated any assets. Idella was not working; it does not seem she was interested in reviving her medical career.

On August 22, 2000, Dr. Hagen contacted the Chatham Township and told them she had killed her parents. At the time of the murders, there was no clear motive.

Trial and Acquittal

The trial started and Dr. Hagen's defense attorney argued for an insanity plea. A psychiatrist for the defense stated that soon after Idella returned to her childhood home she began to experience chronic depression which deepened. She felt like a failure with two divorces and no career, all compounded by the loss of her medical career. She was also worrying obsessively about her parent's health, fearful that her own mental health issues would lead to a need for institutionalization.

Both doctors who testified for the prosecution said her depression deepened significantly in August of 2000. She thought she was hearing voices through TV commercials, traffic lights and playing cards. The doctors also said she heard the voice of a male which she believed to be her father; he was commanding her to kill him and her mother.

The prosecuting attorney pointedly asked both doctors if they thought the killings were considered "patricide-matricide" acts, both equivocally answered no. Dr. Hagen was acquitted of the charges after two psychiatrists testified she was psychotic at the time of the murders.

The judge found Dr. Hagen not guilty on the grounds of insanity and she was remanded to a state mental hospital. He did not order a specific length of confinement, but stated she needed long-term treatment in an institution because she was a danger to society and herself. Under the terms of the law, Dr. Hagen is entitled to have her case reviewed periodically, to see what type of progress has been made.

LUKE WOODHAM

Introduction

Luke Woodham was convicted of murder for a shooting rampage at Pearl High School in Pearl, Mississippi on October 1, 1997. The incident began on the morning of October 1, 1997; Woodham stabbed and beat his mother to death as she prepared to leave for her morning jog. He then drove her car to the school, putting on a long coat to conceal a rifle he was hiding. When he went into Pearl High School, he started to randomly fire the rifle. He wound up killing his ex-girlfriend, one of her friends and wounding seven others before he was disarmed.

Childhood

Luke Woodham was born on February 5, 1981 in Pearl, Mississippi. He had normal parents and an older brother; most would say it was the picture of a typical all-American family. Luke was not beaten or sexually abused during his childhood; in fact his most disturbing memories are of his parents arguing. He always asked his mother when the fighting would stop, and he got his answer one day around the age of eight, when his father left home, never to return.

Life as a Teenager

Luke Woodham labeled himself as a social reject. On the outside, the youngster resembled your average teenager, but on the inside he was anything but that. There is no history of anything traumatic happening in his life, but Luke was simply overwhelmed by emotional issues and unable to cope.

The abandonment by his father affected Luke deeply, and he never fully recovered from the pain. When he was 8-years old, he should have been enjoying his childhood, doing the typical things children enjoy. Instead, he slipped into a deep depression that he would carry with him for many years. Luke was desperate for someone to care about him but it seems nobody did.

Bullying from Classmates

Woodham was a loner, making few friends and was regularly used to being teased. He felt particularly resentful of football players, believing the academics in school, like him, were sorely underappreciated. Classmates taunted Luke for being pudgy, insecure, shy and introverted. It appears the endless bullying he suffered at the hands of his classmates led his anger and rage to fester. Eventually, the teasing and bullying became too much for him to bear. Luke could not take it anymore.

Finding a Place to Fit In

Woodham became a Satanist, joining up with a group called "The Kroth." The group smoked marijuana, and then would sit around talking about the Jewish struggle and the Communist movement for hours. They felt Hitler was evil, but Stalin, Marx and Communism were good. Justin Sledge was Jewish and the mastermind of the organization.

Belonging to a satanic cult gave Luke a sense of belonging, but it was the beginning of the end for this young teen. Grant Boyette and Justin Sledge were co-conspirators of the Pearl High School shooting; both were instrumental in the events leading up to the massacre. Boyette in particular encouraged Luke in his violence, telling him he could win his ex-girlfriend back or get even with her through the use of black magic.

On September 30, 1997, Boyette and Woodham concluded it was time seek vengeance for the cruelty Luke had suffered. After making the decision to act out his homicidal rage, Luke wrote in his journal what many considered to be a sort of suicide note. He wrote that he was done letting the world dump all over him. Hell hath no fury like a mentally unbalanced teenage boy with an ax to grind against the society.

The Day of the Pearl High School Shooting

On October 1, 1997, Luke woke up just like any other day, but it was not going to end well. He armed himself with a .30-.30 rifle, a butcher knife and baseball bat. The first victim he killed was his mother; she died after he stabbed her multiple times, and he also beat her with a baseball bat. Luke then drove her car to Pearl High School where he continued his killing spree.

He entered the school wearing a trench coat, in order to conceal the rifle he had brought with him. Once inside the school, he fatally shot his ex-girlfriend Christina Menefee and her best friend Lydia Kay Dew. Woodham went on to wound seven others during the shooting.

Luke had no plans to stop shooting or hold hostages; he wanted to kill as many people as he could that day. He shot until he heard the sirens of the police; he then ran to his car, planning to drive to the junior high school to shoot more children. However, assistant principle Joel Myrick foiled his plans. The moment he heard shots going off, he ran to his truck and retrieved his Colt .45.

Myrick saw Luke trying to flee the campus, he positioned himself against the windshield, pointing the Colt .45 directly at him. Woodham saw the gun pointed at his head and crashed the car. Myrick approached the wrecked vehicle, subduing Luke when he tried to run away. When Myrick asked Luke why he had shot up the high school, the only response he received was because the boy felt the world had wronged him.

Luke was arrested on October 1, 1997 and was charged with the murder of his mother, Christina Menefee, Lydia Kay Dew and wounding seven others. On October 8, 1997, Delbert Shaw, Grant Boyette, Wesley Brownell, Donald Brooks, Justin Sledge and Daniel Thompson were arrested for suspicion of conspiracy to commit murder.

Trials for Shooting and Murders

There were separate trials for the murder of Luke Woodham's mother and the Pearl High School shooting. Woodham's defense attorney argued at both trials for an insanity plea, saying Luke was of diminished mental capacity at the time of the murders. The trial for the murder of his mother started first, and the jury rejected the insanity plea. Luke was found guilty and sentenced to life imprisonment on June 5, 1998.

The trial for the Pearl High School shootings began on June 12, 1998. During his testimony, Luke stated the power of Satan worshipping gave him the ability to control other people. He openly sobbed when the prosecuting attorney showed the videotaped confession he gave to the police after the Pearl High School shooting. Woodham was found guilty of the shooting deaths of the girls and the attempted murders of seven others.

Once again, jurors at the second trial rejected the insanity plea. Luke was given two life sentences for the murders of Christina and Lydia. Additionally, he received seven 20-year sentences for attempted murder, due to the wounding of seven other victims.

There were conspiracy to commit murder charges filed against Delbert Shaw, Grant Boyette, Daniel Thompson, Donald Brooks, Wesley Brownell, and Justin Sledge. However, the charges against Brooks, Shaw, and Brownell were dropped, because the prosecuting attorney felt it would be difficult to prosecute them. The case against Daniel Thompson was moved to juvenile court because he was a 15-year old minor at the time.

Justin Sledge and Grant Boyette still faced two counts apiece of being an accessory to commit murder. Boyette was convicted and sent to the Mississippi State Penitentiary at Parchman, a boot camp program. He was sentenced to six months; he additionally received five years of supervised probation. The trial of Justin Sledge was delayed, but Judge Barbour eventually handed down a four month sentence for the one people called the "mastermind" of the Pearl High School shooting.

Three days after he was convicted, Luke Woodham was moved from the Forrest County Jail in Hattiesburg, Mississippi. He entered the Mississippi Department of Corrections system on June 25, 1998. Woodham underwent a psychological evaluation while at the Central Mississippi Correctional Facility, in order to be assigned to a permanent facility. As of 2014, Luke Woodham remains incarcerated at the Mississippi State Penitentiary in Sunflower County.

KIP KINKEL

Introduction

    Kip Kinkel is an American spree killer, which is someone who has killed two or more victims in a short time at different locations. On May 21, 1998, he murdered his parents and then proceeded to go on a shooting rampage at Thurston High School in Springfield, Oregon. Kip killed two students and wounded twenty-five others. According to those who knew the family, the Kinkels were a loving and close knit bunch. However, Kip was always struggling with school. He was described as immature, emotionally withdrawn and had way more problems than apparently anyone realized.

Childhood

Kipland Philip "Kip" Kinkel was born on August 30, 1982, to William and Faith Kinkel. Kip attended the Walterville Elementary School in Springfield, and his teachers considered him immature, emotionally stunted and withdrawn. In 1990, Kip's teachers recommended the Kinkel family hold him back for a year, so he was made to repeat the first grade.

By the time Kip entered fourth grade, he was diagnosed by specialists as having dyslexia and was placed in special classes to help him. Kip experienced disappointments and failures early in life; perhaps it weighed heavily on him, because he was born into a family of gifted academics. Kip continued to qualify for special education classes, working with a counselor the whole year.

When Kip was in seventh grade, he and some of his friends used the internet to order some "bomb building" books. Upon being caught, Faith Kinkel began to worry about the type of friends Kip was hanging around with, questioning whether they were a bad influence on her son. In 1996, Kip and some friends got caught stealing CD's from the local store. The trouble continued when he bought an old sawed-off shotgun from one of his friends, hiding it in his bedroom.

Counseling Visits

Kip and a friend were arrested for throwing rocks off of a highway bridge. He was charged for the offense and remanded to the Department of Youth Services in Eugene, Oregon. In response to the rock throwing incident, Kip's parents became concerned about his behavior, taking him to see a psychologist. The boy was diagnosed with major depressive disorder, but the psychologist found no evidence of a thought disorder or psychosis.

Kip and his mother continued to see the psychologist on a regular basis. According to reports, the Kinkels were impressive parents. They wanted Kip to take responsibility for what he had done and to set things right with the victim. The psychologist noted Kip was not the "typical" delinquent child he was used to seeing. He wanted to make amends to the victim and he was genuinely sorry for what he had done. It was determined Kip would do 32-hours of community service, write an apology letter and pay for any damages the rocks had done to the car.

Over the next several months, Kip experienced some troubles but his psychologist felt he was improving. He was put on Prozac, and the doctor noted it helped him sleep better and allowed him to control his temper. By the fourth counseling visit, Kip's doctor noticed he had an ongoing obsession with explosives, but while he remained depressed, he appeared less angry.

His parents were satisfied with Kip's improvements in attitude and temperament. As a reward, William Kinkel took Kip to purchase a 9 mm Glock. The understanding between them was that Kip would educate himself about the gun and pay for it with his own money. He was not to use the gun without his father present, and it would be his on his 21st birthday.

The Kinkels did not mention the purchase of the Glock to Kip's doctor. In his notes, the doctor reported Faith felt Kip was less irritable and in a better mood since he had been on Prozac. At the eighth counseling session, Kip's doctor noted he was getting along with his parents. William was making an extra effort to spend more time with his son.

By July 30, 1997, Kip's doctor wrote he was responding well to treatment, no longer appearing to be depressed. Along with his parents, Kip's doctor believed he was doing well enough to discontinue any further sessions.

More Guns

Kip purchased a .22 pistol from a friend, but did not tell his parents. He entered Thurston High School and according to his parents, he did much better in school. William Kinkel was friends with the football coach, and he contacted Kip at home and invited him to try out for the freshman football team.

By the fall of 1999, Kip had been off Prozac for three months. William purchased Kip a Ruger .22 semi-automatic rifle under the condition he would only use it with adult supervision. It was another gun purchased with Kip's own money. Around the same time, Kip began writing in a journal. He stated that he wished he were bigger, talked about how he hated himself and pondered his loneliness.

From December of 1997 through March of 1998, there were three school shootings in the United States. Kip and a friend were watching coverage of the Jonesboro school shooting and he recalled Kip stating it was "cool." In May of 1998, Kip found himself in trouble again, this time for toilet papering a neighbor's house. He got caught and the next day and had to go clean up the mess.

On May 19, 1998, Korey Ewert stole a .32 caliber pistol from one of his friend's fathers. He arranged to sell the gun to Kip. It is not clear whether or not Kip knew the gun had been stolen, but he purchased it and took it with him to school.

Kip Is Expelled from School

The morning of May 20, 1998 Kip Kinkel went to school with the gun from Korey and $110 in cash. He put the money and gun in a paper bag, hiding it in his school locker. The man who owned the gun, Scott Keeney, called the school to report his gun was missing. He provided the principle with the names of students he believed may have taken the gun, but Kip's name was not brought up.

A detective happened to be at the school and after talking with a few of the students, went to speak with Kip. At 9:15 a.m. Kip was removed from study hall. The detective told Kip he was investigating the theft of a gun from one of the parents. Kip admitted having the gun in his locker, and he and Korey were arrested. As a result of the gun theft, the boys were escorted off school property in handcuffs and suspended from school, facing possible expulsion.

Later in the afternoon, Scott Keeney called William Kinkel when he heard Kip had been arrested. Bill was very upset at what Kip had done, but he was even more concerned with how Faith was going to handle the news.

The Shootings of Faith and William Kinkel

At approximately 3:00 p.m., after William got off the phone with Scott Keeney, he was sitting in the kitchen drinking coffee. According to the confession Kip gave the police, he grabbed the .22 rifle from his bedroom, got bullets from his parent's room and went downstairs. He fired one shot to the back of William's head, killing him instantly. He then dragged the body of his father into the bathroom and put a sheet over it.

At around 6:30 p.m. Faith Kinkel arrived home, and Kip met her in the garage. According to his confession, he told her he loved her and then shot her two times in the back of the head. He then shot her three more times in the face and once through the heart. Kip drug her dead body across the garage floor, placed her in a corner, and covered her with a sheet.

Thurston High School Shooting

On May 21, 1998 Kip got up at 7:30 a.m. and dressed in a long trench coat. He filled his backpack up with ammunition and three guns. He had also taken a hunting knife, taping it to the back of his leg. He drove his mother's vehicle to school, parking it a block away. Kip walked down a dirt pathway, took a shortcut by the tennis courts and through the back parking lot.

He arrived inside the school around 7:55 a.m. and promptly shot the first two of his victims. He then fired off the rest of the ammunition he had, as he walked through the school cafeteria. By the time he was wrestled to the ground, two students were dead and twenty-five others were hurt.

The Aftermath

Kip Kinkel confessed to murdering his parents, explaining in detail how and why he went on a shooting rampage at Thurston High School. On May 22, 1998, Kip was charged with four counts of aggravated murder. He was indicted on fifty-eight felony charges with four counts of aggravated murder on June 16, 1998. On September 24, 1999, Kip Kinkel reached a plea agreement with prosecutors; he pled guilty to four counts of murder and twenty-six counts of attempted murder.

On November 2, 1999, a six-day hearing was held, which included testimony from psychologists, psychiatrists, victim's statements and his sister's statement. After hearing all the information presented, Judge Jack Mattison sentenced Kip Kinkel to 111 years in prison, without the possibility of parole.

ALYSSA BUSTMANTE: TEENAGED THRILL KILLER AND CHURCH GOER

Introduction

William Bradford "Brad" Bishop is a murderer accused of killing five members of his family in 1976. Bishop was once a United States Foreign Services officer, but now he has been a fugitive on the run for more than three decades. In Montgomery County, Maryland law enforcement officials and the community are left to question why a man would kill his own family. It may have been a combination of many different things that drove him to slaughter his family with a ball-peen hammer. However, law enforcement officials are not giving up on finding him until justice is served.

The Early Life of William Bradford Bishop

William Bradford "Brad" Bishop was born on August 1, 1936 in Pasadena, California. He received a degree in history from Yale and a master's degree in international studies from Middlebury College. After he graduated from Yale in 1959, he served a term of four years in the Army counterintelligence division. Bishop is fluent in five languages; English, French, Spanish, Italian and Serbo-Croat.

He joined the United States State Department, where he served in many postings overseas. The last posting William served was at the State Department Headquarters in Washington. He served as the Assistant Chief in the Division of Special Activities and Commercial Treaties.

Family

William was married to a woman named Annette, and the couple had three sons. He was 39-years old and eagerly anticipating a big promotion. William had recently started taking a prescription medication called Serax. The drug was used for treating insomnia and was used for controlling the symptoms of alcohol withdrawal. On March 1, 1976, Bishop learned he would not be receiving the promotion he had long expected, and the rejection set into motion a series of events that changed his life.

The Bishop Family Murders

After finding out about not receiving the promotion he was expecting, Bishop told his secretary he was not feeling well; he left work a short time later. After leaving work, police believe he drove from Foggy Bottom and went to the bank. Once at the bank, he withdrew approximately $400. From there he drove to POCH hardware. He purchased a ball-peen hammer, shovel, and a gas can that he filled at a nearby gas station. He returned home around 7:30 p.m. that evening, after the children had gone to bed.

The police believe the first victim was his wife, Annette. His mother returned home from walking the family dog, and police believe he killed her next. Finally, he snuck in and killed his children while they were sleeping. Each family member was killed with a blunt instrument.

Bishop loaded all of the bodies into the family station wagon and drove to a remote location in the woods of Columbia, North Carolina. Once there, he piled the bodies into a shallow grave, doused them in gasoline and lit them on fire. The next day, park rangers found the mass grave; inside were the charred remains of the Bishop family.

Police Investigation into the Murders

After the murders, William Bradford Bishop seemed to disappear from the face of the earth. Police confirmed his visits to the bank and hardware store where he purchased the items used to murder his family. According to investigative reports, on March 10, a concerned neighbor of the Bishop family contacted the police expressing concern about not seeing them for several weeks.

The police sent a detective to the family home to investigate the matter. Once on the scene, the detective went to speak the neighbor and retrieved a key to the house. As he approached the front door of the home, he noticed blood droplets on the front porch. Upon entering the home he found more blood splattered inside. The detective then contacted the police who came and processed the crime scene. The bodies of family were later identified through the use of dental records.

On March 18 the family car was found abandoned at a campground. The car contained a bloody blanket, and the spare tire well in the trunk was filled with blood. The next day, an arrest warrant was issued for William Bradford Bishop on five counts of murder in the first degree.

Vanished

William Bishop is alleged to have brutally murdered his entire family and then proceeded to disappear. More than 37 years have passed since the crime, but law enforcement officials are still determined to find him. Bishop especially continues to haunt Ray Knight, who was the sheriff of Montgomery County at the time of the murders.

Ray Knight has long since retired from law enforcement, but he still follows leads. He is willing to try anything to locate Bishop and bring him to justice for the cold-blooded murders of his family. He has tried psychics, but they later backed out because of fear. Ray Knight is not the only one obsessed with finding Bishop. Darren Popkin was a former deputy who worked on the case and he is still actively pursuing information.

Knight and Popkin still meet for lunch once or twice a month, reviewing any fresh leads on the Bishop case. Not an anniversary of the family's murder goes by without these two law enforcement officers thinking of the victims, the fugitive and justice. To them, the Bishop murder is like a book with an unfinished chapter, just waiting to be written.

Twists and Turns in the Case

The Bishop murder case has had many different twists throughout the years. Not long ago, it was discovered he had been in contact with at least two federal inmate prisoners. With one inmate, he referred to a female that was an inmate within the North Carolina prison system. The reference made to the woman may corroborate witnesses who reported seeing him with a female not shortly after he murdered his family. Because of the overseas and military experience Bishop had, authorities feel he is no longer in America. After he killed off any ties he had with the murder of his family, it would not make sense for him to remain.

Since William Bishop has been on the lam, there have been countless alleged sightings. In 1978, a friend of the family claims to have spotted him in Stockholm, Sweden. In 1979, Roy Harrell, a co-worker of Bishop, claims to have spoken to him in a restroom while on vacation in Sorrento, Italy. A former neighbor of Bishop claims to have seen him riding on a train in Basel, Switzerland in 1994.

Bradford Murders in the Media

After the initial headlines broke, the Bishop case has been the subject of many articles and news coverage. The case has been showcased on America's Most Wanted, Unsolved Mysteries, and ABC's show Vanished. It has been written about in Reader's Digest and Time Magazine. In 1978, the bluegrass group Coup De Grass recorded a song entitled The Ballad of Bradford Bishop, which was featured on their album "Rhythm and Bluegrass."

Dead or Alive

There are many different theories about Bradford Bishop and where he could have gone after murdering his family. Since 1976, there have been Bishop sightings all over the world in places such as Belgium, Finland, the Netherlands, England, Greece, Germany, Spain, Italy, Switzerland and Sweden. Other theories exist that Bishop died or committed suicide in the Great Smoky Mountains National Park. There are also those who ponder if he defected to the Soviet Union, resuming his career of spying for the government.

Where did he go? Why did it happen? Is he dead or alive? These are just a few of the many questions law enforcement officials want to have answered, but it will only happen through finding William Bradford Bishop. Decades have passed since the Bishop family was murdered and the motive remains unclear. The mystery continues.

Ronald Joseph "Butch" DeFeo, Jr.

Introduction

Ronald Joseph "Butch" DeFeo Jr. is an American-born mass murderer. Despite having what would appear to others as an ideal childhood, Ronald DeFeo grew up emotionally disturbed. He was convicted of killing his mother, father, and four siblings in 1974. All of the bodies were found lying on their stomachs in bed, with no signs of a struggle. Nobody in the neighborhood heard any gunshots fired and the only thing heard was the barking of a dog. It was a crime that gripped the American public and others around the world, inspiring one of the scariest movies ever made, The Amityville Horror.

Troubled Childhood

Ronald Joseph "Butch" DeFeo Jr. was born on September 26, 1951, the eldest son of Ronald and Louise DeFeo. He was the oldest of four children, and his family lived a comfortable, middle-class lifestyle. Ronald Sr. worked at his father-in-laws Brooklyn Buick dealership. He was a domineering, authoritative figure within the household.

Ronald Sr. engaged in constant fights with his wife and children. Frequently, Ronald Jr. was the target of his father's physical and verbal abuse. His self-esteem grew worse when Ronald became overweight in grade school. He began to be taunted by his classmates. As he grew older, Ronald stopped putting up with the abuse from his father, lashing out at him physically when the opportunity arose.

By the age of 17, Ronald Jr. began to use heroin and LSD. He was soon suspended from school for his violent outbursts and aggressive behavior. Ronald's parents did not discipline him for his bad behavior; instead they rewarded him with incentives of cash and gifts. In spite his failing at school, Ronald Jr, was given a job at his grandfather's car dealership, having no expectations placed on him. It seemed to be no matter how much he screwed up, his family bailed him out repeatedly, which only served to fuel his bad behavior.

The Conflicts between Father and Son

Ronald Jr's behavior seemed to become stranger with each passing day. He threatened a family friend with a rifle on a hunting trip and later he acted as if nothing had happened. Ronald Jr. also tried to shoot his father with a 12-gauge shotgun during one of the fights his parents were having. The gun malfunctioned and his father ended the argument, but was very taken aback by the gravity of the situation.

By 1974, Ronald Jr. began to embezzle money from his grandfather's car dealership. In late October 1974, the dealership gave him $20,000 to deposit into the bank. Instead he planned a fake robbery and was going to split the money with a friend. The plan went off perfectly until the police came to the car lot to question Ronald Jr. Instead of remaining calm, he became enraged.

When police suspected him of lying, Ronald Jr. refused to go to the police station to answer questions and check out mug shots. Ronald Sr. started to think his son had more to do with the robbery. He questioned him about not cooperating with police. Ronald Jr. threatened to kill him.

The Murder of the DeFeo Family
On the evening of November 14, 1974, Ronald Jr. had enough of his father and decided to make good on his threat. He removed a .35-caliber Marlin rifle from his secret stash, entered his parents' room, and started shooting them both as they slept. Then he went into his

brothers' room, shooting them both in their beds. Finally, he made his way to his sisters' bedroom, and at point blank range he shot each of them to death.

After the shooting, Ronald Jr. carried on with business as usual and went about his regular routine. After showering for work, he went about disposing of the bloody clothing and rifle. He dumped the evidence in a storm drain on his way to work and once there, he called home pretending not to know why his father had not arrived at work. Feigning boredom, Ronald Jr. left work around noon saying he was spending the day with friends.

He attempted to establish an alibi by telling each person he saw that day he could not reach anyone at his home. By 6:00 p.m. that evening, he phoned a friend and faked surprise saying someone had broken into the family home; shooting his entire family to death. Friends arrived at the DeFeo home, promptly contacting the authorities.

The Investigation

When detectives began questioning Ronald Jr. about who could have possibly murdered his family, he suggested Louis Falini. He told police about an old grudge between the Falini and DeFeo family over some work Ronald Jr. had done for him at the car dealership. He told the police he had been up late watching television, leaving for work early the next day because he was not able to sleep.

Ronald Jr. told police he thought his family was alive when he left for work, then he explained his whereabouts for the rest of the day. Police put him in protective custody and began searching for the murderer. After police did a more thorough search of the family home, Ronald Jr.'s story began to unravel.

Upon searching the home, police found an empty box for a recently purchased .35-caliber Marlin rifle in Ronald Jr.'s room. As the crime timeline came together, it became more apparent to police the murders had occurred early in the morning. The evidence showed the parents and siblings had all still been wearing their pajamas, so it could not have happened earlier in the day. As the facts came together, it put Ronald Jr. at the home when the murders happened.

Ronald Jr.'s story began to change once police presented him with the new evidence. He said Falini had showed up at the family home earlier that morning and put a revolver to his head. He then recounted how Falini had an accomplice. The two drugged him and then went through the house, shooting each member of his family. As the story came apart, police exacted a confession from Ronald Jr. He broke down and admitted to murdering his family.

Trial and Conviction

The trial of Ronald DeFeo Jr. began on October 14, 1975, almost a year to the day of the murders. The defense attorney for Ronald Jr. attempted to enter an insanity plea. Ronald Jr. testified to hearing voices prompting him to kill his family. A psychiatrist for the defense supported the claim, stating Ronald Jr. was neurotic and suffered from dissociative disorder. However, the psychiatrist for the prosecution proved he suffered from antisocial personality disorder, which made him self-centered but still aware of what he had done.

Jurors agreed with the prosecution, finding Ronald DeFeo Jr. guilty of six counts of second degree murder on November 21, 1975. He was sentenced to six consecutive life terms imprisonment and sent to the Green Haven Correctional Facility in Beekman, New York. Since that time, all of Ronald Jr.'s parole appeals have been turned down.

Amityville Horror Legacy

After the imprisonment of Ronald DeFeo Jr., many books and movies came out about the murders. The first book about the DeFeo family murders called, The Amityville Horror: A True Story, was published in September of 1977. The movie focused on a family who lived in the DeFeo home after the murders. It detailed the supposedly true stories of poltergeists that terrorized the family. A movie based on the book, The Amityville Horror was released in 1979; it was very successful at the box office.

What happened to the DeFeo family was no doubt tragic and captured the attention of the nation. However, documentary filmmaker Ryan Katzenbach suggests there may have been two shooters, claiming DeFeo Jr. did not act alone. New evidence is currently being investigated, but whether or not it has any bearing on the burden of guilt on Ronald Jr. still remains to be seen.

EDMUND KEMPER

Introduction

Edmund Kemper III was an American serial killer who enjoyed killing, dismembering and having sex with his dead female victims. Known as the "co-ed killer," Edmund began his criminal career by murdering his grandparents when he was 15-years old. Later, he killed and dismembered six female hitchhikers. He then murdered his mother and her friend, before turning himself over to the police. He gave law enforcement a full confession of his crimes, telling them in detail where he had stashed the bodies. Kemper was known for his immense physical stature, standing 6'9 and weighing more than 300 pounds. He also boasted above average intelligence, having an IQ of 140.

Early Life and Childhood

Edmund Emil Kemper was born on December 18, 1948. Known by the nickname "Big Ed," he was the middle child and only son of Edmund and Clarnell Kemper. When he was a child, Edmund was extremely smart, but displayed antisocial behavior. He acted out weird sexual fantasies with his sister's dolls and had a dark, twisted imagination.

Edmund grew up being close to his father and was extremely distraught when his parents divorced in 1957. After the divorce, he was primarily raised by his mother in Helena, Montana. The two had a tumultuous relationship because Clarnell was a violent alcoholic who would belittle her only son. It was rumored his mother had borderline personality disorder. She made Edmund sleep in the basement for fear he would wind up raping one of his sisters.

Kemper ran away from home in the summer of 1963, winding up in Van Nuys, California to find his father. Once he arrived, he learned his father had gotten remarried and had another son. Edmund lived with his father, stepmother and brother for a time, but was soon sent back to Montana because his father could not deal with him. Clarnell was not willing to let Edmund come back home, so he was sent to live with his father's parents.

The First Murders

On August 27, 1964, Edmund was with his paternal grandparents living on their ranch in North Fork, California. He was not happy about the move. People tended to shun him, finding him strange. Edmund had grown sick and tired of begin ignored, and people around him only made the situation worse.

Kemper did not like how Clarnell was treating him, and his grandmother was less than kind to him too. People were always pushing him around, and as a result he began fantasizing about killing and mutilating. As a child,

Edmund began to torture cats. He buried one alive, dug it back up, cut its head off and impaled it on a stick.

On that particular August afternoon, Edmund and his grandmother had a heated argument in the kitchen. He displaced the anger he had towards Clarnell onto his grandmother. It did not take much to get him to snap. He grabbed a rifle, and she told him not to go outside shooting birds. He turned around without a word and shot her instead. A bullet hit Maude in the head, and he then shot her two more times.

When his grandfather came home, Edmund heard the car outside. He went and looked out the window, making the decision to kill his grandfather in that moment. As the elder Edmund got out of the car, Kemper raised his rifle, shooting him before he even made it into the house. He then hid the car in the garage, feeling he had avenged the rejection of his parents. Confused about what to do next, Edmund phoned his mother in Montana and told her what he had just done. She advised him to call the police.

The Aftermath of Murdering His Grandparents

Edmund was remanded to the Atascadero State Mental Hospital at the age of 15. He eventually became friends with his psychologist, later becoming his intern. It was at this time his IQ was revealed to be 136. Later in adulthood his IQ was tested at 145. When he was released in 1969, he had grown to 6'9 and weighed 280 pounds. Against the advice of several doctors, Edmund was released into the care of his mother.

After demonstrating he was sane and functional, Edmund's juvenile record was expunged. He went on to work a series of menial jobs, before he secured a job with the State of California Department of Transportation.

The Santa Cruz Hitchhiker Murders

In May of 1972, female hitchhikers in Santa Cruz, California began disappearing. Between 1972 and 1973, Kemper embarked on a killing spree, picking up six female hitchhikers and driving them to a remote area, where he killed them. After shooting or smothering the victims, he would take the bodies back to his apartment and have sex with them. He would often go hunting for a victim after having a fight with his mother.

The Murder of Clarnell Kemper
After killing the six female hitchhikers, Edmund turned his rage towards his mother. While most experts feel his previous killings were a rehearsal for killing his mother, the explanation Edmund later gave police was completely different.

On April 30, 1973, Kemper had planned on waiting for Clarnell to come home from a party, but instead he fell asleep. He woke up a short time later to hear her rattling around in the other room. He went into her room; she was seated on the bed reading a book. She berated him for interrupting her and chastised him. He in turn beat her to death with a claw hammer.

After spending some time having oral sex with his mother's severed head, he used it as a dartboard. He mutilating her vocal cords and put them into the garbage disposal. Edmund then contacted his mother's best friend, Sally Hallett, inviting her over to the house. When she entered he strangled her and left the scene.

Kemper drove east, leaving California and driving through Nevada and Utah. After hearing news about the killings on the radio, Kemper stopped at a phone booth in Pueblo, Colorado. He called police and confessed his crimes, but they did not take him seriously, telling him to call back later. Several hours later, he called the police back and asked to talk to an officer who he knew. He did not talk about murdering the hitchhikers and instead confessed to the murder of his mother. He then patiently waited by his car until the police arrived to arrest him.

The Trial of Edmund Kemper

On May 7, 1973, Edmund Kemper was arrested and charged with eight counts of first-degree murder. His defense attorney offered an insanity plea, but he had his work cut out for him because of Kemper's detailed confession. Kemper was diagnosed as psychotic, but despite being declared safe by his psychiatric record, he had not been cured.

While waiting to go to trial, Edmund tried to kill himself two times, but was not successful. The trial started on October 23, 1973, with three court appointed psychiatrists finding him sane. Dr. Joel Fort reviewed Kemper's juvenile record, testifying to the court about Edmund's previous acts of dismemberment, animal mutilation and cannibalism.

After a one month trial, Edmund Kemper was found guilty of eight counts of murder. He asked for the death penalty, but instead received life imprisonment, with no possibility of parole. Edmund Kemper remains incarcerated in the general prison population at the California Medical Facility in Vacaville, California.

Aftermath

Kemper may have been completely aware of what he was doing and relished in the killings.

Edmund's anger started early in life; the rage was compounded when he was separated from his father. Edmund Kemper is a rarity among serial killers in that he freely offered a detailed account of his crimes, mentality and fantasies. Despite how troubling his revelations were researchers are thankful, because it helps to learn more about the development of a sexual predator and serial killer straight from the source.

www.ingramcontent.com/pod-product-compliance
Lightning Source LLC
Chambersburg PA
CBHW020256030426
42336CB00010B/793